500 DESTINATIONS TO AVOID

and 500 to visit

500 DESTINATIONS TO AVOID

and 500 to visit

BY DR IAN WILSON

CHAIRMAN AND FOUNDER
OF WEXAS INTERNATIONAL

 A **WEXAS** publication

500 Destinations to Avoid first published in London in 2000 by WEXAS International, 45-49 Brompton Road, London SW3 1DE, UK (Telephone 020 7589 0500, Fax 020 7589 8418, email mship@wexas.com, website www.wexas.com)

© WEXAS International 2000
ISBN 0-905802-10-1

The right of Ian Wilson to be identified as the author of this work has been asserted by him in accordance with the Copyright, Designs and Patents Act 1988

The views expressed in this book are those of the author. Individuals should always endeavour to obtain current information on their own journeys. The author, editors and publisher cannot accept responsibility for any loss, injury or inconvenience sustained by any person using this book

Cover design by Wylie Design, London
Printed and bound by Legoprint SpA, Italy

ABOUT THE AUTHOR

Ian Wilson was born in Edinburgh and grew up in New Zealand with a yearning to travel. After university in New Zealand and Oxford, where he gained a DPhil in political philosophy, he did a brief spell in advertising with the J Walter Thompson Company before launching WEXAS in 1970. His home is in New Zealand ('the last refuge in an ever more unpleasant world'), where he spends most of his time when not travelling or looking after WEXAS. His interests revolve around surfing, diving, sailing, skiing and collecting early maps of New Zealand.

OTHER BOOKS BY IAN WILSON

The Influence of Hobbes and Locke
500 Tips for the Long Haul Traveller
Trouble-free Travel - an Insider's Guide
Black Jenny (a novel)

CONTENTS

INTRODUCTION page 9

CONTENTS

INTRODUCTION

Has the world really changed in the last 20 years or is it just me? The places that used to be so-called adventure destinations are now over-run with Western package holiday-makers and many of the elements of mass-market tourism. It's not just Goa. Increasingly it's places like Marrakech, Kathmandu, Bali and half a dozen destinations in Thailand.

Then there's the personal security issue. Am I getting paranoid or has the world really got more dangerous for the Western traveller? What about Egypt, Kenya, Chechnya, Yemen, Uganda, Nepal, Cambodia? Does a spate of tourist massacres and hostage-taking signify anything worth worrying about? Maybe I'm getting soft.

But whatever happened to those wonderful overland journeys of the Sixties and Seventies when it was a doddle to get hold of a Land Rover, head across Turkey, Iran, Afghanistan and Pakistan to India, sell the vehicle in Bombay (I can't bring myself to write Mumbai) and, after 'doing' India, travel through Penang and Singapore to Australia?

That was then. The world was your oyster. Now that oyster seems to have turned a little bad.

Maybe I have only myself to blame. I started WEXAS in 1970 and it has grown since then with the never-ending expansion of travel. The world shrank each year. Airfares came down and down in real terms. Travel guidebooks helped to pave the way - backpackers first, with the package holiday market waiting in the wings for it all to be safe enough for the less secure to venture out of their European cocoon and taste a bit of the exotic life.

This book will ruffle a few feathers, since it's stuffed with my personal opinions and many sweeping generalisations, particularly about the way things have changed for the worse.

Most of the places I have been to I would not revisit. That doesn't mean going there was a mistake. It just means they weren't special enough to lure me back a second time. My likes and dislikes are the stuff of this book and some of them won't be your own cup of tea.

I've been travelling the world since 1953, when I was nine years old and sailed round the world to New Zealand in an ocean liner, almost the only way to go then. I haven't been everywhere since, but as Chairman of WEXAS and Publisher of *Traveller* magazine, I've had the chance to visit many countries, most of them in the developing world and some well off the tourist trails - places like Mauritania, Sao Tome, Principe, Mayaguana, Rodrigues, Cocos Keeling, the Admiralty Islands, Sainte Marie, Nuku Hiva, Fogo, Maio, Flores, Fernando de Noronha, to name a few of the lesser known places that you'll find in this book.

I feel as though I haven't even scratched the surface of the globe. There are glaring gaps in my travels. Since I love the sea - the warmer the better - I have seen very little of the interior of Asia. And since I prefer what I call 'real sea' - the stuff with waves - I haven't spent a lot of time around the Middle East. In this book you will find many references to beaches, surfing (my lifelong passion), diving and sailing.

You will find my dislike for cities outside Europe, and my love of off-the-beaten-track places where there are as few other Westerners as possible. This being so, you will not often find me waxing lyrical about destinations where there are lots of expensive places to stay.

Before I start being criticised for a Eurocentric approach to travel in the developing world, I had better own up and confess that I have come full circle. I studied anthropology for a year in the Seventies so that I would be able to do my job at WEXAS properly. I went down the road of promoting responsible, low-impact tourism - leave your prejudices at home, learn some of the local language and a smile will go a long way if you don't - that kind of thing. It made travel easier and more pleasurable. I travelled with my kids from when they were three months old and they turned out to be a better ice-breaker than any amount of smiling and uttering the local words for 'hello' and 'thank you'.

But in the end I realised I had prejudices I would never shake off. It was all very well understanding that if local people were unfriendly it was because they were exploited by colonial powers, or they envied what I so obviously possessed, or they couldn't understand when I tried to make them speak my language, or the presence of a Western visitor was enough to make them feel somehow injured and inadequate through no fault of their own. Despite understanding these things, I still clung to my prejudices, and you will find them in this book when I say that the locals are unfriendly, or Bangkok is unbearably polluted, or Nairobi is no longer a safe place if you're white.

One thing though - I now no longer make arrogant assumptions about being a 'traveller' rather than a 'tourist'. Such a distinction is in your eyes only. To a Sri Lankan Tamil woman earning the equivalent of one dollar a day picking tea in one of the big plantations, there is no difference. It has often been said in a well-meaning way by Westerners - pretending to put words in the mouths of such local people - that it would be a good idea if travellers would stay at home and send their money instead.

Implicit in this is the idea that all tourism corrupts local culture and does more harm than good. That the money brought by tourism (if it rubs off on the local people at all) is a good thing and some kind of compensation for the cultural damage that tourism is deemed to inflict. As every serious student of anthropology soon learns, a visit by an anthropologist to a remote tribe leaves that tribe changed for ever. Tribes are not museum artefacts. They will change anyway, simply changing all the faster if brought into contact with the West.

INTRODUCTION

I've often noted that the happiest people I have seen in developing countries are those with least contact with the outside world. It's not that so-called development makes people unhappy, nor the loss of traditional values as such. It's rather a question of that Western disease that we see in our own society through advertising and the celebrity culture - people are taught by the media to want things which they never knew existed. In the impact of tourism on the developing world, we are seeing a parallel phenomenon. People are exposed to Western wealth and values and end up wanting these things for themselves but unable to have them. In comes frustration and out goes happiness.

So when I say that the locals are unfriendly in such and such a place, what I am really saying is that they are no longer happy because the Westernisation of their world has left them frustrated and I am a reminder to them of what they would like to have but never will. Even that may sound arrogant, making me the cause of so much unhappiness. There must be other reasons. Or maybe I have just mistaken the failure to return my smile as something else. Is it any wonder that in Islamic countries, in particular, America is seen as the great Satan? The Westernisation of the world is inevitable, warts and all, just as English is becoming the world's common language by degrees. Like it or not, you cannot turn back the tide. As travellers or tourists or whatever we call ourselves, we can only go on travelling responsibly, hopefully aware of our prejudices, but prejudiced nevertheless.

The traveller of today is undoubtedly more cynical and self-seeking than he or she once was. We're concerned for our personal safety as never before, thanks to a growing number of incidents that have involved the death of tourists. Whole swathes of Africa are now written off in many people's minds, as well as a large chunk of the Muslim world, particularly Algeria and Egypt.

So we wonder whether it's safe to go to Uganda or El Salvador. And at the same time we worry less about a McDonald's in Kathmandu, or a fishing village in Goa wiped away for the sake of Mr Big's next three-star hotel. Just as we've become desensitised to violence on TV at home, we've become desensitised to our own negative impact on the developing world. Maybe it's just me. Or maybe we're really so concerned now about our own pleasure and our own safety that we would rather think about what our Lariam anti-malarials are doing to our brains than whether it was right or wrong to look the other way as we passed a woman with a starving baby holding out her hand as we passed her by.

Travel makes many demands on us. Some of them are demands on our conscience. The auspices for the next century are not good. In the West we have become inured to violence and suffering. The world is increasingly polluted. Finite natural resources are depleted inexorably. And we travellers - we tourists - go on taking what we can get for ourselves and call it a holiday.

Don't judge me too harshly, therefore, when I talk of travelling in a rental car, hermetically sealed from the local environment, or of staying at a big hotel. The next day I will be off to some place where such comforts will be only a memory.

This book is not a guidebook. Here are my very brief, personal and sometimes cynical impressions of many of the places I have been to. For me, some are to avoid and some are to visit, and most are a mixture of the two - go here and do this, but avoid this place in such-and-such a country and go to that place instead. These are only my opinions and I would be sorry if you agreed with them all.

Too many travellers follow the flock, which is why there are still so many wonderful places to discover for yourself if you leave the flock behind.

I have paid my dues in the course of almost half a cen-

INTRODUCTION

tury of travelling and now I want to share some of my impressions with you, however personal they may be. After all, I'm chairman of a travel company and it's my professional duty to suggest places to go and places to avoid.

Here, for what it's worth, are my thumbnail sketches of some of the places I've been to - the good and the bad.

Chapter One
AFRICA

MOROCCO

I must like Morocco or I wouldn't have been back there five times. Of all the Arab countries, it's the one that offers real surfing, especially the big waves around the Agadir area in winter. But Morocco has much more to offer visitors. I'm not wild about the heat in summer there, though I like the country during the rest of the year. In the High Atlas, villages like Ouazazate, with its tiny streets and white houses, is a curiosity worth a day's visit. In fact just driving through the Atlas Mountains in spring or autumn is a treat.

Further south, the cities of Marrakech and Fez are worth a day each, if only for their vast souks, provided that you can say 'piss off' convincingly in French or Arabic to the hordes of boys who will plague you with offers to be your guide. If you cannot drive them away, the next best thing is to hire the toughest and most persistent, and pay him to drive off the rest.

My first memories of Morocco from the Sixties are of hordes of dogs and small boys trailing around the outskirts of rubbish strewn towns. Each subsequent visit has shown signs that things are getting better and there no longer seems to be absolute poverty in Morocco - just poverty - so some of that tourist money must be filtering down. Fortunately, there is also less sign of the homosexual paedophilia that was once such a blot on the landscape in the days when gays in Europe remained in the closet and only came out in places like Morocco.

Morocco is many things to many people. To me it is the fascination of the markets, and especially the leather goods made from the hides of goats and camels. But there are other interesting things in a Moroccan market - the piles of dried dates, the incense, the melons in summer sold for next to nothing.

Go south to Taroudant, the Moorish town that rises like a citadel from the desert, if only for the sight of the place as you approach. Do not expect to see Tuareg, the 'blue men' of the desert, there these days. They have almost all been assimilated into mainstream Moroccan society.

There is Morocco and there is Spanish Sahara, which was once Spanish territory and is now part of Morocco, after many years of fighting between the Polisario (the Sahara freedom fighters) and Morocco, ostensibly over territory pure and simple, but in reality over the minerals of the area, especially phosphates. The drive of several hundred miles down the coast to the old Spanish Foreign Legion fortress town of Dakhla is like a step into history if you have ever read the books of the French writer Saint-Exupery. This was the territory he flew in the Thirties to deliver the mail, and subsequently as a fighter pilot in the Second World War. I drove all the way in a hire car from Hertz in Agadir, staying at the few fishing villages along the way. The road follows the Sahara coastline and there is little to see except desert, a few camels and a worryingly large number of old rusting freighters shipwrecked along the coast. Here and there along the way are army roadblocks, reflecting the fact that potentially this is still disputed territory.

Morocco has three major coastal towns on the way south before you reach Spanish Sahara proper. There is Sidi Ifni, which was once quite a nice place, I believe, when the Spanish still had it. Now it is decrepit, its old seafront promenade crumbling. Further south is Tan Tan, which used to be the last place in Morocco before the southern boundary was redrawn. This is now a sleepy coastal village where the atmosphere is not good and the sea is dangerously rough a lot of the year.

Further down the coast is the uninteresting port of Tarfaya. Despite such isolation, it is curious to consider the fact that the busy package holiday destination of Fuerteventura in the Canaries is only some 80 miles away across the water. Then, a little further south, there is Laayoune, a town a few miles inland from an unbelievably ugly port area used for the shipment of phosphates. Laayoune itself has a certain charm and one gloriously faded hotel of the type you still sometimes run into in India and Sri Lanka - a reminder of how things probably looked 60 years ago. In a town like this, you are quite likely to be the only visitor from Europe.

And after that there is a coastal village every 50 miles or so, usually with a simple place to stay above a simple restaurant serving the ubiquitous *tajine*, the Moroccan stew of meat or fish with vegetables.

In Dakhla itself, a garrison town with fortified walls built by the Spanish, visitors must report to the police station on arrival. There isn't much to see or do here except admire the waves crashing into the cliffs and wander around feeling conspicuous as the only European traveller, in all likelihood, within 100 miles. About 200 miles to the south is the border with Mauritania, but at the time of my visit the army blocked any further advance to the south of Dakhla. Now, apparently, the Moroccan army organises an armed guard twice a week to lead vehicles in convoy down to the Mauritanian border.

Tangiers is not what it was and is best missed. Casablanca is a decrepit coastal town where Morocco's richer Europeans tend to live. But Rabat, the capital of Morocco, is a good place to visit the market and spend a night. Rabat is as Moroccan as Casablanca is European. Do not expect in Casablanca to find reminders of the famous film of the same name. The film was all shot in a studio in the United States and bears no resemblance to the real Casablanca.

EGYPT

I have made two brief visits to Egypt - so brief that I have never been further afield than Cairo and the pyramids. I did manage to fit in the Cairo Museum on my whirlwind trips and found it happily chaotic, a far cry from the ordered environment of the Egyptian section of the British Museum. The pyramids, though, tend to disappoint, if only because most photographs give the impression that they are floating out there somewhere in the desert, whereas they are right bang next to one of the poorest quarters in Cairo, and this you only discover on arrival. Still the pyramids weren't built to please tourists and neither were the city's slums. One of the least pleasant features of the tourist experience at the pyramids is the hassles with touts, guides, souvenir photographers and the like. Someone must like it, though, or they wouldn't be there. Read Mark Twain's account of his trip there and you will find that nothing has changed.

MAURITANIA

This rates as one of the weirdest places I have been to. For one thing the wind never seems to stop blowing in Nouakchott, the capital, and it blows sand everywhere, into every nook and cranny of every house. The less poor (there are no really rich people in this Islamic republic) spend a lot of money trying to hermetically seal their houses and pay people to spend their lives sweeping sand out of the garden. Everything is sandy. The centre of town is ramshackle and the only substantial building seems to be the bank. This country is seriously poor.

A few miles away is the coast, and when you reach it you will expect to find the hotel that is shown on some maps. It is quite hard to locate, as it is almost totally buried in sand. It looks as if the effort to sweep the sand away finally became too much. I had hired a four-wheeler to travel with driver and cook to the coastal town of Nouadhibou, about 100 miles or so to the north. This is the second largest town in Mauritania and there is no road between the two towns. The only way to travel between them, unless you fly, is by driving up the beach at low tide, preferably in a four-wheel drive vehicle. Vehicles tend to do the trip in a convoy, usually overloaded, so that if one vehicle gets stuck in the sand, others can pull it out. We saw one stuck truck with about 50 people in it, so it must be a regular occurrence.

However, the beach doesn't go the whole way and there are many miles of driving across desert sands. Forty miles south of Nouadhibou we saw four teenagers stuck in the sand in a two-wheel drive vehicle and rescued them from a certain death in the tropical sun.

But the best thing about the coastal drive, apart from the fact that the wind doesn't always blow as you go north, is camping by the shore, eating grilled fish round a campfire. At night jackals prowl around your tent. The bones of camels bleach in the sun. And millions of locusts swarm over the ground, getting crushed in their thousands beneath the wheels of your vehicle.

The sea is spectacular though the water can be surprisingly cold in winter considering how far south this is. There is one so-called national park along the way - the Banc d'Arguin National Park, a birdlife sanctuary with little to see as all the birds are on islands offshore and whenever the wind is favourable for a trip out there on one of the local fishing boats, the birds take off. When they return, there is no longer any wind to get you to the islands, so the birds lead a very undisturbed life. It was in this area that we spotted four foreigners, the only other Westerners we saw in Mauritania except for one Frenchman in Nouadhibou.

We crossed the railway line into Nouadhibou that hauls the longest train in the world, a string of ore-carrying waggons that stretch, they say, for over half a mile. Transport on this is free if you're willing to sit on top of the ore in the sun. There are no passenger carriages.

A few miles from Nouadhibou we encountered a border post where there was no way the guard was going to let us through without a bribe. I offered him the 50 ballpoint pens I had been saving to give away to child beggars. He took these and still demanded money. In the end our driver forked out and we moved on into the town a few miles ahead.

I liked Nouadhibou. The influence of the Foreign Legion was here too, though don't ask me if it was the French or the Spanish version. The fort virtually on the border with Morocco was manned by an officious captain in the Mauritanian army who refused to let us drive through to the shore. We surfed a mile to the south instead and I broke three ribs on a hidden rock. That meant two days of agony before I could get a flight back to Nouakchott and out. Pain-killers made the going easier and allowed us to still see something of this strange place. There are freighter wrecks along the coast, and hundreds of wrecked boats off Nouadhibou itself. A small promontory is home to the last remaining Atlantic monk seals in the world and they swim happily in the water 100 yards or so from where kids play in the waves.

Nouadhibou has a few cheap restaurants and a hotel that takes in tourists and organises fishing trips. Mauritania's limited appeal to the outside world is based on game-fishing out of Nouadhibou and bird-watching around the national park area on the coast. I would have stayed in Nouadhibou for longer, were it not for the accident. It enabled me to do a bit of freelance work on the Mauritania section of Footprint's West Africa guidebook, and I was even offered the job of Mauritanian consul in London if I wanted it. I politely refused.

SENEGAL

Mauritania's neighbour to the south is really two countries ethnically and physically. The north, which includes the capital Dakar, has much in common with the Maghreb countries to the north, while the south - the Casamance - is black African and actually a lot more interesting than the north. Not that the drive between north and south is easy, especially in a two-wheel drive vehicle.

Down the coast, south of Senegal's nation-state enclave that is Gambia, the area known as the Casamance is a big draw to French tourists in the winter, especially the area round Cap Skiring, with its Club Med. The locals are extremely friendly and their favourite pastime is wrestling. The beaches of the Casamance are safe for swimming though a bit tame for surfing. They are usually calm, whereas in the north, surf of up to three metres is the norm.

Dakar is not a friendly place, nor a particularly safe place if you believe in hanging on to your possessions. Head for the Casamance if you go to Senegal at all.

GAMBIA

I wouldn't go back here if you paid me. This tiny enclave of a country tucked into the coast of Senegal has become the only West African country besides Senegal to have a developed tourist industry. So much so that it has a Swedish-language radio station and endless hotels strung along its one windy beach. The beach and hotels are the haunt of local gigolos who spend their lives hustling female tourists for sex, or selling tacky souvenirs. Package tours fly in and out of here from all over Europe, including the UK. What the brochures don't tell you is that there is a permanent plague of tsetse flies on the beach. These insects, though they won't usually give you sleeping sickness, have a nasty bite and make any kind of enjoyment of the beach all but impossible. This isn't the real West Africa at all, and for some sun and surf in the winter I can think of a dozen better places to go.

Ivory Coast

It's said that Ivory Coast has the highest standard of living in black Africa, and that may very well be true. They're very proud of the skating rink at the Intercontinental Hotel in Abidjan. On the other hand, the capital has little to offer the visitor and is best departed unless you like skating or football, the local obsession. Along the coast there are no real tourist hotels, but there is the odd guesthouse and, this being a former French colony, there is occasional good food to be had, especially seafood. I travelled on local buses in Ivory Coast, having flown to Grand-Bereby, and found a rabble of friendly locals to talk to and answer questions about the surfboard I was carrying (a nightmare on a crowded vehicle among the screaming chickens). The water was warm for swimming and there were no sharks, which is a good thing if you are going for a swim or a surf, but a bad thing if you are diving and like a bit of excitement. The water seems to be permanently cloudy in West Africa, so you would not want to snorkel here anyway.

Ghana

Ghana is my favourite country in West Africa. I was there at a time when there had just been a revolution and there were only five Europeans in the country. Beer was very hard to come by. I travelled in the company of a local guy who had a taxi and was the same age as me. He needed a bit of hard currency to buy car parts and as he and I got on well, he showed me Ghana and I paid him about £20 in sterling at the end of the trip. We both were mightily pleased with our deal.

The trip of several days took us up the coast to Cape Coast, Takoradi and beyond, staying anywhere we could and eating what we could, as hotels and restaurants outside Accra were non-existent. In fact, they were almost non-existent in Accra as well. There was only one place to go for a drink in the evening, and that was Nero's, a nightclub dive where five hookers would dance with you in return for no more than a smile.

To the east of Accra we crossed the chaotic border into Togo, car and all, presenting a renewal notice for the car's insurance as the logbook, which, needless to say, was back in Accra. At first, when the border guard pretended to read the document, though it was upside down, I was amused. On reflection, though, I can see that I was simply applying my Eurocentric sense of humour to a situation that really isn't funny at all. Literacy is one of the many problems facing this struggling continent.

The people of Ghana were desperately poor at that time, but never short of a smile.

Togo

I only got to see Lome, the capital, and visit the nearby beach, which went on for miles and seemed to be devoted to oil refining and export. Apart from that it seemed like a mile from the top of the beach to the water, though it was probably only 400 yards. A nondescript place with little to draw the visitor's attention and probably best avoided, unless you have something to offer this impoverished country, as did the Peace Corps volunteers I met there.

Liberia

A pity that Liberia has fallen apart in the last few years. When I was there, it was a few weeks before the first revolution, in which the President was shot in his palace and then the entire Cabinet were tied to posts on the beach and used for live target practice by the rebels for the next three hours. As the president had spent an entire year's GDP on his palace, it was hardly surprising.

Monrovia, the supposedly exemplary home of freed American slaves after emancipation in the US in the 1860s, was a strange place at the best of times. It had the best music radio station I have ever come across - possibly something to do with the fact that Liberia was always a crossroads of American black and African culture.

I stayed at the Intercontinental, the archetypal citadel hotel on a hill and possibly the inspiration for the expression 'fill the bath - it looks like civil war'. I almost got shot there, since I refused to pay the bar bills of the two previous occupants of my room. Even the manager tried to insist that I was liable for the unpaid debts of my predecessors, though the bills were plainly signed by others and carried a date when I wasn't even in the country. In the end I slapped down in cash only what I genuinely owed.

The manager called the hotel guards and I walked out to my taxi accompanied by my wife, with two automatic rifles pointing at my back.

We were heading up the coast to Robertsport. Though we were not fully aware of what was going on, the country was close to flashpoint and the dictator-President's grisly death was only a short time away.

On the way, we were stopped by the secret police under the command of an articulate viper who clearly had his eye on my wife and the attractive wife of the American who had joined us for the ride.

We were made to empty our suitcases while the three revolver-carrying gangsters sized up their chances of raping the women and murdering all four of us. Only one thing saved us in the end. We were going to stay at a hotel along the coast at Robertsport set up by a German. By chance we knew that the President and this

27

German were friends. We feigned close friendship with the German, emphasising his good relations with the President. The articulate leader of the three got the message and decided against rape and murder. He called off his goons and we escaped.

It was only when the revolution occurred a few weeks later that we realised how close a call it had been. The President's secret police - all those who did not manage to escape - were tortured and put to death in the popular uprising.

We went on to windsurf at Robertsport - a strange thing to be doing, it seemed, in such an odd country. At the Tubman Museum in Robertsport, the curator had not been paid for six months and we helped him out by giving him $20 in return for a stone burial artefact.

I'm not sure if I did the right thing. But I am fairly sure that the entire contents of the museum were looted subsequently.

Back in Monrovia I walked half a mile to the beach carrying my surfboard, followed by some 500 or so local people, who lined the beach to watch when I paddled out. That evening we went for a bizarre Chinese meal at the only Chinese restaurant in town. The food was good, but what was memorable was the interior of the restaurant. We ended up hidden behind velvet curtains deep in the interior of this strange place where every table seemed to have its own private cubicle.

Liberia rates up there in the half dozen strangest places I have ever been to. I cannot see myself going back, but it is a place I will never forget.

GABON

What a disappointment Gabon turned out to be - especially after paying about £40 for a visa. This is a country with a President called Bongo who has enriched himself and, to a lesser extent, his country by exploiting the rainforests for timber. Vast areas of forest have disappeared as a result. Go to Port-Gentil expecting to find beaches and all you will find are logs strewn all over the shoreline and not a spot worth swimming at. There is one pleasant cafe on the shore with friendly staff and that is about all I can say that is good about this place. Drive to the coast some ten miles away and you will find the beach untempting and the sea swept by powerful side currents. Not a lot of fun.

At the main hotel in town, the local Forte, phone calls had to be the most expensive in the world. The starting rate for a local call was about £15 per minute and you needed a mortgage to call overseas. No surprise, then, that not only was sending faxes expensive, but here they also charged you to receive them. The hotel food was terrible (especially for a francophone country), the service worse and the staff dishonest. I wouldn't go back to Gabon if you paid me.

SAO TOME AND PRINCIPE

If there was one good thing about Gabon, it was that you could fly from here to Sao Tome, a bizarre former Portuguese colony far out to sea in the armpit of Africa. This place was a welcome relief after Gabon. There was a comfortable small hotel to stay at, the food was good and the locals tolerably friendly in the old town with its market reeking of smelly fish. You could safely change money on the black market at a place behind the market where hustlers plied their trade. The police seemed to turn a blind eye, and even the bank itself advised me to go to the street changers for a better rate. (It's only a little bit better, which is why this free exchange market is tolerated.)

There are a few pretty beaches around the island, and reasonable snorkelling. The only hassle we had was from a guy who pestered us on the beach, and he came from Cabo Verde, so our positive view of the locals remained unsullied.

By far the prettiest part of the island is also the least accessible. The staff at our hotel reckoned we could not reach Porto Alegre at the southern end of the island in a car as small as a Suzuki jeep, even though it was four-wheel drive. The vehicles that made the trip over the horrendous mountain road once a day were six-wheel drive trucks - and the road surface in places has boulders bigger than a football. In the end we made it, though there were precipices as well as the road surface (or lack of it - some of it was a river bed) to contend with.

It was worth it. There are a couple of villages by the sea at the end. Then there are pretty white sand beaches that could be anywhere in the Caribbean, which is saying something if you are at all familiar with the cloudy water and yellow sand that is the norm down the west coast of Africa.

These spots were idyllic and almost unvisited by outsiders, partly owing to the inaccessibility of the area, and partly due to the fact that tourists are such a rare commodity in this country. The best of them is known locally as Praia Piscina.

Principe lies about 80 miles away from Sao Tome and is completely different. Most of the people here have never been to the main island that makes up the other part of their country. The only way to see this island is to go round it in a small boat, which is what we did, completing the journey in about two hours, before stopping to snorkel at a spot alive with a school of small barracuda.

There is one very expensive hotel on Principe (Hotel Bom Bom) and one guesthouse in the town of Santo Antonio. We got a freebie at the former and then stayed at the latter. The expensive hotel caters almost entirely for big game fishermen, for this place teems with black marlin at the right time of the year. We met one fisherman who had just caught eight marlin in seven days.

A couple of miles from the hotel, on a high plateau overlooking the sea, is all that remains of a once-thriving plantation house. Now the few remaining inhabitants of the surrounding hamlet (the house itself being a ruin) are cared for by an Austrian Catholic priest, a young man with a flowing beard that adds decades to his age. He welcomes visitors and told us about plans to turn this simple island into a huge billion-dollar free port catering to the whole of West Africa. Hopefully it will never happen. Such development would shatter the local community on this pretty island, however much it brought in work and money.

There are nice beaches on this coastline: one of the best spots is in front of another old ruined plantation house, which is said to be haunted by the ghost of a woman who once lived there who was raped and murdered by her disaffected workers. Visitors should not expect coral here. The water is clear, there are lots of fish to see, but coral is missing, underwater rock formations making up for it instead. Overall, Principe would not compare as a dive spot with many better known places. It is best regarded, like the larger and more populated Sao Tome, as a curiosity that still reflects some of its Portuguese past and has escaped the attention of most of the rest of the world.

SOUTH AFRICA

I've only been to South Africa twice and don't claim to know it well, especially as my last visit was in 1985 - they declared a state of emergency the day I arrived. What I do remember most is picking up hitchhikers - black and white - as I drove from Durban to Jo'burg then down to Cape Town. People said I was crazy to pick up black hitchhikers, but at that time it was relatively safe.

I would not find it so safe now, with the collapse of law and order since the demise of apartheid. This must inevitably be viewed as a part of the price to be paid as South Africa recovers from its past. However, crime in African cities is not something limited to South Africa, and places like Nairobi and Lagos, which never experienced apartheid, only colonial rule, have serious urban crime problems.

The seafront around Durban looks good in all the photos. The reality is tawdry and disappointing, like a poor copy of Copacabana, right down to the mosaic promenade.

Jo'burg is best driven through without stopping. Keep your doors locked. They say you should not stop at red lights in the city unless you have to. East London and Port Elizabeth reminded me a lot of bits of New Zealand years ago - old-fashioned in a pre-war kind of way that has probably kept it safe, I imagine, from the worst of the crime wave.

Even Cape Town, which used to consider itself safer than Jo'burg, is beginning to feel the effects of the crime wave. For all that, Cape Town is rightly considered one of the most beautiful cities in the world. What this means is that the coastline is beautiful, as anyone who has ever driven around it will have seen for themselves. It is a pity therefore that the sea, which looks so enticing, is very cold all year round. You can just about manage to swim in January and February, but it's wetsuit country the rest of the year, in complete contrast to the sea around Durban, which is warm and pleasant all year round.

So Durban has the warm water and Cape Town has the scenery (though the interior around Cape Town is no big deal). Apart from that, the Cape means vineyards and wine, seafood restaurants and Table Mountain for the best view of all.

Worth one visit at least for Cape Town, before it all gets out of hand.

MADAGASCAR

This huge island is far enough offshore to be really different from continental Africa. It's relatively isolated and extremely poor, as a walk around the market area of Antananarivo, the capital, will soon make clear. The market is said to be the second largest in the world. Certainly it's vast. I spent a few hours combing it out of curiosity and saw no sign of the thieves and pickpockets who are reputed to be a part of the action there.

The striking thing about Madagascar is that for all its coastline, it has not got much in the way of pretty beaches. I thought Fort Dauphin in the south sounded interesting but it turned out to be a big disappointment, though I did get to see a hammerhead shark swimming past while I sat on my surfboard. Fort Dauphin is the jumping off point for Berenty, famous for lemurs in the wild. This is worth a day trip, though there is a lot of hypocrisy about feeding the lemurs, as you would hardly see any if people weren't in the habit of breaking the rules and feeding them.

Tamatave on the east coast is a dull place with an interesting market which sells local strawberries grown in the high country. They are not, however, worth buying, being almost completely tasteless, unlike the strawberries of that other tropical island Sri Lanka, which are slightly more flavoursome and to be found in the market in Nuwara Eliya high in the tea country.

An abattoir empties offal straight into the sea to the south of Tamatave and there have been enough fatal shark attacks in the area (usually tiger sharks) to keep almost everyone out of the rather cloudy water these days.

From Tamatave you can fly to the island of Sainte Marie about ten miles offshore. Taking the ferry is not a good idea in any case, as they tend to overload it and it has been known to capsize in mid-channel.

AFRICA

Sainte Marie is the best thing about Madagascar. In fact, in many ways it feels much more like being in the Seychelles than in Madagascar, despite the geography. The island is pretty and slow moving and has several places to stay, the best of them in the north. True, the beaches at these hotels are not amazing and to get to good beaches you have to walk about ten miles, as we did, to the north-east coast. Here we were disappointed to run into one other traveller (the only other we saw that day), a German girl who was doing voluntary work in Madagascar and was on holiday from the mainland for a few days.

The beaches of the north-east coast of Sainte Marie were spectacularly wild and probably dangerous if you went swimming outside the sheltered lagoon area. However, there were giant pools, refreshed with each tide, to laze and swim in, and the surroundings, rocky with palms, were postcard perfect. Even the local people, who live in tiny thatched huts and are clearly very poor, were delightful, especially the many children who were curious to talk to us with no ulterior objective, so it seemed. It's amazing the spots you can find if you're prepared to walk ten miles. This was shortly before Jacques Cousteau died, and the day we walked to the sea, we decided not to join a group from our hotel going by boat into the channel in the hope of seeing humpback whales calving while being filmed by Cousteau's team from the *Calypso*. When we heard that the group had been able to snorkel and watch a baby humpback being born, we were envious, there was no denying it.

We finally spent a few days further north on the east coast of Madagascar, at a place called Sambava. There we stayed in a comfortable straw-roofed chalet and drank the place out of fresh fruit juice. A long beach stretched in front of us, but it was disappointing. The sea was no good for surfing, the water was cloudy and the side currents were too strong to be safe for children. The sun was scorching too.

I don't like hot weather, especially if it's very humid. If I go to hot countries it certainly isn't for the heat, though I like warm water. Sainte Marie rates with me, but not much else about Madagascar, except the markets and the lemurs.

TANZANIA

Dar es Salaam is a city without any redeeming features that I could spot. We headed for the Ngorongoro Crater and some wildlife, then Arusha national park, where a large number of elephants and giraffes appear to have been shoe-horned into one very small space. Of the two areas, Ngorongoro is by far the more impressive. Don't go to Tanzania for a beach holiday on the mainland coast or you'll be disappointed, though I hear Zanzibar, Mafia, Pemba and other islands more than make up for this.

KENYA

They have just abandoned the visa charge for Kenya for UK citizens, which is a sign of the times. Kenya had it too easy for too long as a tourist destination, and finally its weaknesses are catching up with it. For a start, there's the growing crime rate, not just in Nairobi but up and down the country. Much violence is aimed at tourists these days and a number have been killed. When I was in Kenya in 1972 there were said to be 100,000 elephants in Tsavo National Park. Their number is now said to be about 5,000.

The coast of Kenya is undoubtedly pretty, at least at places like Kilifi and Watamu. However, somewhere like Malindi, even in 1972, was unattractive and overrun by Germans, most of them there for the prostitutes in the pre-AIDS days. Street crime was already a problem in Nairobi back then, and private armed guards were a feature of all coastal properties of any substance. I have not gone back to Kenya since those days, as stories filtered back about how the place had gone downhill and was getting worse. The government seemed corrupt (no surprise in Africa) and I reckoned that eventually people would wake up and realise that there were better places to see game in the wild than Kenya. Basically this place gets a big thumbs down.

CHAPTER TWO
LATIN AMERICA

ARGENTINA

Buenos Aires

You could be forgiven if you mistook the centre of Buenos Aires for central Lisbon or Madrid. There are impressive European-style buildings and wide boulevards. This is the only city in the southern hemisphere that resembles a European city to any degree. There are pleasant sidewalk cafes, but it's at night that BA is at its best. The central streets fill with young people doing what young Latins love to do best - walking around in groups looking at each other, flirting with their eyes. You can still see this appealing and old-fashioned interchange between the sexes in the less touristy parts of Spain and Portugal, though even there, regrettably, it is disappearing under the unstoppable tide of American values.

Take the usual big city precautions and you should have nothing to fear in the streets of central Buenos Aires. In that, too, this city is different from others in South America. Only central Santiago seemed to me to be equally safe. Perhaps it is no surprise that the other cities of this continent, especially Rio de Janeiro and Bogota, but also Lima, Caracas and Sao Paulo, should be ridden with street crime, much of it violent. The difference in BA and Santiago may be to do with the uniformity of the racial mix. These are semi-European cities, especially in the centre, without as much of the *mestizo* and mulatto elements to be found in cities further to the north. Where populations are racially mixed, there seems to be a higher propensity for crime the world over. In the southern part of South America, where there were never many indigenous tribes to begin with, and most of these, sadly, were wiped out by Western diseases, the prevalent genotype is Hispanic, with a strong element of Italian in Argentina.

Apart from that, Buenos Aires has polo and barbecues, both a matter of considerable national pride.

Mar del Plata

The rich of Buenos Aires cross the River Plate to Uruguay when they want to go to the beach - to the (arguably) smart resort town of Punta del Este. The poor, as always, stay at home, and the middle classes head for Mar del Plata, where the Plate finally becomes ocean about 200 miles south-east of Buenos Aires. You will not find foreign tourists in Mar del Plata, and if you go there in the December-February period you will probably not find the sea either, as the beach stretches a long way out and has more deckchairs covering it than you ever thought possible. Go in March or April, however, (but not at Easter) and the beach is yours alone. The sea is still a long way off, the water is cold and, in fact, there is little to excite the imagination. Even the concrete promenades, looking like a poor imitation of the local resorts north of Lisbon, have little to offer except endless mass-market eateries and endless examples of that staple of South American cities, the ice cream parlour. (Though South American ice cream is generally excellent, with the best to be found in Lima.) Basically I wouldn't go to Argentina for a beach holiday. The beaches south of Mar del Plata are little better than those in town, though they have the advantage of being almost empty most of the year.

PERU

Lima

One thing struck me above all about Lima - everywhere you go the place seems dusty. In fact it is dusty. Lima is built in the middle of the Peruvian coastal desert and it shows. I found nothing to keep me in Lima, though admittedly the Humboldt Current that flows up the west side of South America makes the coastal waters some of the richest in the world for fishing, so you can be sure of good seafood if you pick the right restaurant. I wandered around the centre near the Parliament building and was reminded by a friendly local that if I wanted to hang on to my watch, I should button down my shirtsleeve.

Driving to the beach in Lima was a bit of an adventure. We found the once famous Waikiki Surf Club at Miraflores, formerly the hang-out of the spoilt sons and daughters of the rich. It looked as dusty as everywhere else. So we tried for a beach further north. We knew we were getting close in the *barrio* to the north, but we never made it. The place was getting more like a shanty town the further north we drove. We had the only car in sight and we were getting more and more attention as the streets narrowed and people began to hem us in. Maybe we misjudged the threat of a carjacking, but discretion prevailed over valour and we turned around and headed back the way we had come without even stopping.

South of town we found a more accessible beach, but even here it looked as though the car would not be safe for five minutes if left. That was Lima. We checked out of our hotel - one of those ones where you feel you are in an oasis and it doesn't feel morally right with all the dust and poverty round about - and headed north up the Aztec Highway, which is the Peruvian part of the Pan American Highway.

Trujillo, Chicama and the Aztec Highway

Dunes as big as mountains is the impression you get along this barren coastline, interspersed with shanty towns built of packing cases, each proudly surmounted with a TV aerial. The town of Trujillo, with its statue of the genocidal Pizarro, is worth a passing glance before heading further north. I was bound for Chicama, reputedly the home of the longest surfing wave in the world. There we stayed at the Sony Hotel. Despite the many enterprising Japanese who have settled in Peru, including the President, this was no offshoot of the electronics giant. My six-year-old son and I got the only room with a view - and a loo that had to be flushed by filling a bucket at the well in the courtyard. Dinner was at the restaurant across the road - fresh crab *ceviche*. The table was a packing case. The floor was beaten earth. The waiter put a live crab on my plate, smashed it over the head with a rock and poured lime marinade on top. Voilà - crab *ceviche*. Well I like crab *ceviche* - or any kind of *ceviche* if it's well made, but this was a little extreme. Then again, can you complain when dinner costs 20 cents?

Cuzco and Machu Picchu

Aero Peru were pretty desperate, even as Third World airlines go, but we got to Cuzco in one piece and promptly suffered from mild altitude sickness - nausea and headache, and a loss of breath every time you walked uphill. Take it easy for 24 hours though, and the symptoms go. It was good to be in clean air under blue skies and Cuzco deserved a day's visit to the church, market, etc. Don't expect the Indians to smile and chat, though. Throughout South America you are reminded of the legacy of the Spanish conquistadors and their bloody search for El Dorado. Everyone with a European face is treated as an honorary Spaniard by the Indians. It's a pity, but can you blame them? If you do manage to take the time to get to know the Indians of Peru and elsewhere, overcoming their natural reticence and suspicion, I'm told they are warm and welcoming.

Machu Picchu is known from photographs the world over. You get there by walking for four days or you take the train from Cuzco, as we did, a few years before it was bombed by Shining Path guerrillas. It's a putt-putt kind of train and on it there's the chance to chat with other travellers. The ancient Inca city of Machu Picchu is grand and its stonemasonry remarkable, especially if it's swirling in clouds as it was the day we went there. There are almost no Indians to be seen. Virtually all the other people you will see will be visitors, though fortunately not too many .

This stone-built citadel is on a par with the pyramids and the Taj Mahal - touristy in one sense, but something you have to see - preferably before they build a big resort hotel currently on the planning board.

ECUADOR

I would have to admit that Ecuador was my favourite country in South America.

Quito

The capital city sits high on the *altiplano* and the drive up there from coastal Guayaquil is breathtaking. It was built in the sixteenth century by the conquistadors after they had slaughtered the local people in the name of God. They built a city that is remarkable now for its many early churches. In fact, a visit to Quito is really a tour of some of the best of Latin American church archi-tecture of the sixteenth and seventeenth centuries - heavy baroque with a great dose of candles, saints and shrines - Roman Catholicism at its most ornate and primitive. The thing I remember most is going round the cathedral and finding Mark, my (Protestant) six-year-old son on his knees, praying before the image of a saint.

Apart from that, it has to be said that Quito appears to

be comparatively safe if you take the usual precautions about what you wear, where you go and when.

Otavalo

There is one village about 30 miles north of Quito that is worth a visit, and that is Otavalo. Here the Indians in the market are friendly and will sell you llama and alpaca knitwear for a few dollars. The village is pretty and the surrounding countryside even better. In fact you could be forgiven for thinking you were in Switzerland in summer - it has that *Sound of Music* feel about it. There are lakes with windsurfers, mountains on the horizon and green and grassy meadows. Not what you'd expect in South America right on the equator.

Guayaquil and the coast

This is Ecuador's main coastal city. It's brash where Quito is staid. The fruit markets are cheap, the churches are gaudy, illuminated by saints with electric candle crowns. It's probably not as safe as Quito, but I didn't have hassles. It's not somewhere to stay for more than a day or two, but it isn't big and oppressive like so many cities that make you want to leave the moment you arrive. Drive out to the coast from Guayaquil and you'll hit it at a place called Salinas. Neither here nor further north is the coastline interesting or attractive, though locals flock there at weekends. The water is warm, however, the local seafood is good and cheap and the general feel of the area is relatively safe.

Galapagos Islands

You can reach the Galapagos by flying from Quito or sailing from Guayaquil. We chose to fly and from there sailed on the *Tip Top*, the small yacht owned by

LATIN AMERICA

Rolf Wittmer of the Wittmer family of Floreana (a German family featured for their eccentricity in all histories of the Galapagos) . Most people who visit these islands do so in a cruise boat, and the trip becomes a bit of a safari park expedition. The nice thing about having your own boat is the chance to go where you want to go, and as I wanted to snorkel and surf as well as see the wildlife, the *Tip Top* would have been ideal, apart from the fact that the skipper was surly and didn't like to have passengers who decided where they wanted to go. So we went where tourists didn't go - places like San Christobal (excellent surfing) - and had a strange conversation with an alcoholic American who had been living there for 40 years (every tropical island should have one, and many do, usually on the run from Uncle Sam's Internal Revenue Service).

We saw the island of Isabella, but not the giant tortoises. We went snorkelling only to find the visibility poor - the wrong time of year. Not even a Galapagos shark in sight.

On Santa Cruz, the main island, we walked from Puerto Ayora four miles across the rocky shore to reach a white sandy beach inhabited by a solitary seal. The capital's discotheque, though, didn't register on the Richter scale and dancing was limited to the paso doble. On Espagnola we saw the birds and iguanas and I discovered how dangerous it can be to surf among female seals when a bull sea lion surfaced three feet from me and made it clear I wasn't welcome among his harem. Finally on Floreana, a barren rock of an island where the few inhabitants speak German rather than Spanish, I was collared by the Wittmer matriarch and given a letter to post when back in England. It was nice to see an old custom of the colonial world alive in this day and age.

Yes, the Galapagos are worth a visit. Go before it's ruined. Visitor numbers have doubled since I was there, and money and bent politicians - rather than the interests of endangered species - now dictate development.

Brazil

Rio de Janeiro

Rio gets mixed reviews, mainly because it's the most dangerous city outside Panama City and Colon that I have ever been. Everywhere are stories of theft, violence and murder, and they don't seem to be exaggerated.

The beach at Ipanema is stunning and the bodies beautiful. Leblon Beach to the south is better still. The surfers hang out at Arpoador just south of Copacabana, but the legendary beach itself is a bit of a disappointment. The mosaic promenade is dirtier than it looks in photos, there are touts on the make everywhere and behind the glitzy facade of all those seafront hotels, the town is pretty dingy and uninteresting.

Go to the sights to see them once - Sugar Loaf Mountain, the giant Christ of Corcovado, Copacabana. Drive down to Leblon Beach. You will see inland the hillside *favellas* - the slums where a wise man would not set foot. I don't normally do any shopping when I travel (all that extra luggage to haul half way round the world). However, there is one good place to buy in Rio and that is at the weekend leather market. Buy the top of the range stuff and you will find that the quality is good and the prices, after some bargaining, are excellent value for money.

If you go anywhere at night, take a taxi. Walking in the daytime in the main parts of the city is usually safe, provided you keep your wits about you. I only got accosted by a potential mugger once in the four days I was there. Someone in the group I was with managed to have a gold chain torn from their neck. A woman had refused to hand over her valuables in our hotel a few weeks before we arrived and had been pushed off the balcony on the eleventh floor. In the same hotel that year, the

45

night staff had all been tied up while two masked men systematically plundered the guests' safe deposit boxes. And that's just the tales from my personal acquaintance.

I wasn't in Rio for Carnival and I wouldn't want to be. Spectacular it may be but the thought of crowds like that is enough to send me rushing for another desert island.

Fernando de Noronha

Brazilians rave about this place and no one else in the world has heard of it. They call it the Galapagos of the Atlantic. It's an island about 150 miles out into the Atlantic from Recife in northern Brazil. Planes go there daily and tourism is strictly of the eco variety - very controlled. For instance, you cannot go there unless you have accommodation booked in advance. I went there with an Argentine friend. We pre-booked at a local guesthouse, meals included.

The locals have cottoned on to the fact that demand outstrips supply on their tiny island, and charge an arm and a leg for a bed, and meals that would make your average gaol food feel like the Ritz.

That said, it's the water that's the problem - not the quality of it but the fact that the drinking stuff is so rationed that it's cheaper to drink Coca-Cola. We found ourselves begging for second helpings of water at meal times, and as we were each paying about £70 per day for meals and a shared room in which a cat couldn't swing a cat, we rapidly began to suffer from dehydration. We tried the one local store for bottled water. 'Sorry - sold out.' Any Coke? 'Sorry, just sold out.' It wouldn't have been such hot work if we'd caved in and rented a jeep for about £100 a day. But you could walk round the visitable half of the island in a couple of hours (the best half was out of bounds, courtesy of the military) - so we walked, getting thirstier and thirstier.

So why do the Brazilians describe this lonely Atlantic island as Heaven on earth? (They really do rave about it.) Well, it's a marine national park. There are admittedly beautiful sandy beaches and one spectacular mountain peak. The water does contain some interesting fish and the odd shark. But I snorkelled a lot while I was there and, apart from the rather poor visibility, I've seen much better marine fauna in 50 other parts of the world. I had to come to the conclusion that the Brazilians who raved about this place had never been anywhere else to compare it with.

The water was warm. There were free films (in Portuguese) in the visitor centre every evening, and this provided a meeting point of sorts. I didn't mind the shanty town feel of the one village on the island. The people were friendly and there was no crime. I could even live with the terrible food. It was the water problem that ultimately turned me off.

Not a place I will go back to, but if the drinking water problem is ever solved and if the right season of the year is chosen for underwater visibility, I would have to say Fernando could be worth a trip - say four days max.

CHILE

Santiago

Chile's capital is fairly safe but also pretty boring. If you like an endless variety of fast foods made of meat, though, this is your place. The cathedral is not the prettiest of Latin American churches and the market is not to die for. There's a feeling of traffic pollution in the air on a hot day and the rich people all live on the hill. The restaurants are unexciting and, frankly, the best thing to do in Santiago is get out. I haven't been to Mendoza, centre of the wine-growing area of that name, but I'm told that it's a beautiful easy-going town with a lake, so you could head out there on the train if you're underwhelmed by Santiago.

NICARAGUA

This tiny country has had a lot of bad press in recent years, what with the civil war and the Contras and the US covert involvement (remember Colonel Ollie North?) That all ended quite a few years ago. Go to Nicaragua today, though, and you'll be hard pushed to find a single American visitor. It's as if, for Americans, the war is still going on. Americans are funny like that when it comes to travel. One incident and that country is finished for the next 20 years.

Anyway, I took pleasure in visiting Nicaragua without Americans, or precious few other foreign visitors, come to think of it. There's nothing more enjoyable than visiting a country where you are one of very few outside visitors - the people are almost guaranteed to be friendly, and in Nicaragua they usually are. That's not to say that Nicaragua hasn't got its problems. It's still desperately poor. It was fortunate to be spared the hurricane that devastated Honduras and Guatemala in 1998.

Like Costa Rica, Nicaragua is in a sense two countries - a western part that is Spanish/*mestizo* and an eastern part that is Caribbean, with a largely black population. The eastern part of Nicaragua, which I have not visited, is said to have more in common with the eastern part of Costa Rica (which I have visited) than with the western part of Nicaragua.

Managua, the capital, is a sprawling urban mass of low-cost, low-rise buildings. Much of the centre, which was flattened by an earthquake in the Seventies, remains flattened. The cathedral, a modern building (Managua is not an old Spanish city), is boarded up to this day. So if you visit Nicaragua, head out of town as soon as you can, preferably the same day.

There are two old Spanish cities you can visit -

Granada in the south and Leon in the north (though distances are short in western Nicaragua and the furthest points by road are no more than three or four hours away).

Leon was well worth the visit. I had to get a missing bolt made up for the fin of my surfboard and my attempts to find help around the city led me to a succession of friendly people all willing to point me in the right direction. Leon was built in the sixteenth century and, from the look of it, was never as rich as Granada. The buildings are smaller and it doesn't have the same enticing courtyards at the centre of every house. But the feeling of the place - I can only describe it as that - was warm, safe and friendly. The people are distinctly Central American *mestizo*. The place is busy with activity spilling onto the streets in the way it must have done in Europe in the Middle Ages. The Pacific Ocean is half an hour's drive away at a place called Poneloya, where there are warm waters and cheap eateries and places to stay. (We're talking $5 a night for a room with a relatively primitive but functioning bathroom in the corner and a view of the ocean straight out the door.)

Not all the Pacific coastal spots in Nicaragua are appealing, and many are best avoided at the weekend, when families from the cities descend on the coast, as they do in neighbouring Costa Rica. However, the weekend hordes seem to delight in following each other like sheep. They like to have crowds around them on the beach, so if you can find somewhere secure to park, it's easy to find a beach to yourself 20 minutes up or down the coast.

The city of Granada is more attractive to look at than Leon. But I didn't get the same feeling there. It still felt relatively safe, even in the evening (only Managua is probably dodgy at night in western Nicaragua), but there weren't the same smiles when you caught the local's eye - more a feeling of indifference. That's fine. There's no reason why the locals should smile back because some *gringo* is smiling inanely at them. It's just that in Leon the people really did seem to be smiling. Maybe I imagined it. Anyway, Granada is the jumping-off point for the volcano island of Arenal in Lake Nicaragua, famous for its Indian handicrafts and legendary Indian settlements. I stood and gazed at it from the shore, but felt untempted to take the ferry over and spend a day or two there as most visitors to Nicaragua do. Perhaps it was this familiarity with visitors passing through which had made the people of Granada that much less friendly. Whatever the reason, I gave Arenal a miss.

If you have been to next-door Costa Rica, as I had on an earlier visit to Central America, you cannot help but compare the two countries. Costa Rica is dripping with North American and European visitors. It's greener, more luscious than Nicaragua. The beaches are more accessible yet mostly not too crowded. There are restaurants and accommodation everywhere you turn in Costa Rica. Yet in some way I preferred Nicaragua. I suppose if I'm honest about it, it was simply the fact that I like to get away from crowds of other foreign visitors and in Nicaragua there was definitely the feeling of having the place all to myself.

However, there was another point. Nicaragua has the reputation of being dangerous. There are stories of guns left over from the civil war and of carjackings. English friends living in Costa Rica were to have joined me in Nicaragua, but pulled out at the last minute, alleging that it was too dangerous. Well, I went to Nicaragua and drove around on my own in a Toyota Land Cruiser and had no problems. On the other hand, while I had been in Costa Rica two years earlier, two German tourists had been kidnapped for money, and a busload of tourists had been marched from a bus at gunpoint and systematically robbed. And yet Costa Rica is supposed to be the safe place, the so-called Switzerland of the Caribbean.

The real gem of a place in Nicaragua is the small fishing port of San Juan del Sur, only 20 miles of empty beaches north of the border with Costa Rica. And to the north of San Juan stretch miles more of empty beaches. Most are reachable after a rugged drive (four-wheel drive is definitely recommended) and I had no problems leaving the car parked in this area - it was so deserted that not only were the beaches empty, but also most of the surrounding area.

San Juan had about 20 foreign visitors when I was there. The locals descend on the place at the weekend, giving it a party atmosphere - bearable, even fun for a couple of days. There's a string of seafood restaurants (open air) along the curve of the small beach, and there are at least a dozen cheap places to stay in town. We're talking up to $15 a night for a room ,and about $5 for a seafood meal with a *cerveza*. As a general rule, prices for meals and accommodation in Nicaragua are about half their equivalent in Costa Rica, which itself is still something of a bargain. You could happily spend four days in and around San Juan del Sur if you had a car.

Nicaragua is definitely somewhere I would go back to, if only for Leon and San Juan del Sur. But first I plan to visit El Salvador, also the victim of a bad press, to see if the stories are true or whether, after all, it's a relatively safe place to visit.

COSTA RICA

Costa Rica has a lot of what North Americans, in particular, are looking for in a getaway destination - it's relatively safe (except possibly on the Caribbean side), it's relatively cheap (though it's already twice as expensive as neighbouring Nicaragua), it has miles of pretty unspoilt beaches, there's lots of restaurants and accommodation to choose from, including a few luxury hotels, and the people and the cops are fairly friendly. You'll notice I'm saying 'fairly' this and 'fairly' that. That's because Costa Rica is moving to the point where it's getting too popular for its own good, and remember the rule - the best places, the safest places with the friendliest locals, are places where there are fewest visitors from the moneyed outside world. So has Costa Rica got a future as a nice place to go, or even to live (thousands from Europe, the USA and Canada have already built holiday homes there)? The answer is a qualified 'yes'. Much will depend on the future of the tourist infrastructure at this crucial stage. Unfortunately, it's the point at which most Third World governments get it wrong, on the grounds that more is better.

The pattern is simple, yet I have never seen any Third World government able to spot this pattern, let alone do anything about it. The story goes like this. You get a number of well-heeled visitors, drawn by the fact that the place is not yet spoilt. The government, especially if its ministers have got their fingers in the till (they usually have), like what they see, so they start promoting their country heavily overseas. More tourists come, only they are not the ones with a lot of money looking for a secret refuge. What the welcoming government ministers have failed to realise is that their original visitors, who found their way to their country without the come-on of an ad campaign and a thousand tour brochures, were all there was of that kind of market. Any extra visitors from the donor countries (if we can call them that) inevitably come from further down the scale. So the new lot arrive and the smaller, richer, older lot leave as a result. The government doesn't even realise this has happened until it's already over, but they wouldn't care anyway as the volume of the new visitors brings in more money than the small group of rich visitors ever did. Thus is a country turned from upmarket tourism to mass-market tourism. It happened in Kenya. It happened in Barbados. Kenya, in particular, has lost my respect.

Even so, all this would be all very well except that it

has one big negative consequence. Limited upscale tourism brings in money but limits the negative impact that comes with all foreign visitors. Mass-market tourism, to put the problem in simplistic terms, means a greater level of negative impact. Poor Third World peoples are affected by tourism in many ways, whether the money brought into the country does or doesn't trickle down to them. Add to this the fact that mass market tourists have less cultural empathy (if I can call it that) when abroad, and you can quickly see what happens when a government in a place like Costa Rica, liking the effects of early tourism, decides it wants more of the same. The problem, as I've just explained, is that they will get more, but not of the same - only worse. And that is the risk that Costa Rica faces at its present turning point.

San Jose

Forget it. It's not an old colonial town. It's relatively safe if you're careful, but there's not much to see except a lot of cars.

The Caribbean Coast

Costa Rica's Caribbean population is largely black, being the descendants of indentured labourers brought in from Jamaica late in the last century to build the railway line from San Jose to the Caribbean coast. The main town on the east coast is Limon, a shabby place where the feeling is definitely not good if you bother to stop and walk around (don't even contemplate it after dark). Most tourists heading for the east coast, many of them surfers, end up staying in one of the cheap places around Puerto Viejo. Here the atmosphere is warm and friendly and crime relatively petty, what little there is of it. There's a disco by the sea, open to the air, that everyone heads for in the evening. There are innumerable eateries from cheap to very cheap. It can rain a lot at times, as I know from experience, having spent a day under teeming skies in January. The beaches are not much to write home about, compared with the more familiar beaches of the Caribbean that most of us know from visiting the Leeward or Windward islands. In fact, though I liked the shanty village laid-back feel of Puerto Viejo, I wouldn't rate it worth going unless you were there to surf its famous reef (Salsa Brava). In many respects it has the feel of Kuta Beach in Bali about 30 years ago, before it really started to get developed. There's always the expensive turtle farm hotel to the north near the Nicaraguan border, but that's where the two German tourists got kidnapped. (Actually it was eight, but they kept two for several weeks, both women, and let the others go.)

The Nicoya Peninsula

The Pacific coastline of Costa Rica, though not very long (I would guess about 200 miles as the crow flies), divides into three distinct areas: the Nicoya Peninsula in the north, the central coastal area and the Osa Peninsula in the south. Much of the far north of the Nicoya Peninsula is unreachable except by four-wheel drive vehicle.

The best known spot, and one definitely for the overseas market (as is most of the peninsula really), is Tamarindo. It's not cheap by Costa Rican standards, the local beach is nondescript and I cannot see the point of staying there when there are plenty of better, more isolated places to stay, provided you have a four-wheel drive. We didn't, and we paid the price in punctures in our two-wheel drive. If you count a dozen or more rivers that we drove through, we were lucky to make it all the way south down the peninsula's coastal route - a distance somewhere around 100 miles at a guess.

I won't spoil it by telling you about it - but yes, go and find the empty beaches for yourself as we did. There are miles and miles of them, and yet you are never more than ten miles from somewhere to stay. In the south of the peninsula the scenery is great - birds, monkeys, and Costa Rica has to have the most colourful trees I have seen anywhere. Most visitors don't venture down into the deep south of the peninsula. If you do, you'll be almost alone, even in high season (winter), and you won't regret it.

The Central Coast

This is where the locals go to the beach, but there's a lot of it and they tend to stick, as always, together. In fact, half of San Jose descends on Puntarenas at the weekend. There you will find families, several miles of them, spread out along the beach under awnings over tables, having their picnics and throwing balls around. Better to move on and leave them to what they like doing best - being with thousands of other Costa Ricans. After Puntarenas there are miles of empty beaches interspersed with small townships (the big towns are inland, up on the plain) that are really just tourist developments. One that used to be charming years ago, but is now totally ruined by overdevelopment and tawdry discotheques, is Jaco. If you do go here, you will find places to eat and to stay, but forget about the beach. It is beginning to show signs of pollution and you will be far better off staying in a place like Dominical and exploring the empty beaches around.

The Osa Peninsula

For some reason this part of the coast always seems to be hotter by far than the rest, and this was the main drawback. The other is that the price of accommodation and meals here is at least double that of the rest of the country. The reason is not hard to find. After the small town of Puerto Jimenez, there are no shops. In fact, after a while the splendid road (especially splendid compared with the potholed affairs that pass for roads in the rest of the country) becomes a track and then ceases to exist. By then you will have gone past half a dozen lodges designed for the upper end of the visitor market. They are all aimed at one thing - walks in the Corcovado National Park.

Here there are rumoured to be jaguars, though I doubt if many tourists have seen one. What you will hear is the eerie sound of howler monkeys, and with luck you will see a whole flock of scarlet macaws. The beaches in the national park are attractive, and they are almost always empty. The accommodation at most of the lodges is fairly basic despite the high prices, and you could come away with a feeling of having paid too much for what you got. But the peninsula that is Osa is big and virtually uninhabited and it's my guess that in the next 20 years there will be major tourist development in the attractive area to the south of the park's borders. There will be no development inside the park itself. Overnighting there is forbidden and visitors are encouraged to stick to the trails. Is Osa worth it? Yes, definitely, but be prepared for the heat and try to go at the coolest time of the year.

PANAMA

Panama City

This is a very big city. I was surprised at how big. It can also be dangerous, as I found out walking the streets of a distinctly black quarter at about 11 in the evening (with a friend, looking for something to eat) and got mugged. It was my fault. I had my guard down. We fought the attacker off and he managed to escape. So did we, back to our hotel a mile away before he came back with his friends. The incident left a nasty taste as we had just arrived in the country that evening and were due to be there for a week. When we drove through the busy port area by the waterfront market, we got a distinct feeling that this too was dangerous, as we got hemmed in almost to the point where the car could not advance. We locked the doors from the inside and got out of there fairly quickly.

Then we began to hear stories about Colon, the main town over on the east (Caribbean) side of Panama. According to one guide book, visitors to Colon had a 95% chance of being mugged in their first 24 hours there. Nice. So when we went there, we only stopped for petrol. We did not get mugged. What we saw of Colon looked like a bigger version of the town of Limon on the Caribbean side of Costa Rica, about 50 miles up the coast. We did, however, stop in historic Balboa, where Spanish ruins dating from the sixteenth century are to be found - and not much else. The nearby Caribbean beaches were particularly unappealing, though some of the countryside was pretty.

Panama City is not a place to hang about. It has a fairly elegant seafront and the city stretches for miles behind it. The Canal Zone, which we drove beside, is Little America, a town in itself, self-contained as only the Americans know how. But we were interested in the real Panama, up the Pacific coast. We were not too disappointed. It was not like Costa Rica. It was not like Nicaragua. For one thing, attribute it to drugs or the Yankee dollar or Canal revenues, this country had money. Big shiny 4WDs were everywhere. There were police roadblocks every so often and, while we didn't get beaten up, they definitely hadn't been to Swiss finishing school.

LATIN AMERICA

The hinterland

Were the people friendly, away from the big cities? Generally not - not as friendly as in Costa Rica and definitely not as friendly as in Nicaragua. This was a country that didn't rely on tourist dollars for its wealth, and tourists were few and far between. That should have made the people friendly, according to my theory. Maybe it just made them more independent, or more equal economically. We met friendly surfers and friendly Chinese running a roadside restaurant, and a friendly man in a pharmacy who sold me Fucidin antibiotic ointment - the traveller's panacea - available only on prescription in the UK.

I came away from Panama with mixed feelings. In Costa Rica and Nicaragua, the main risk of street crime is on the east coast where the population is basically black. The crime situation in Panama is slightly different. The black, or more accurately mulatto, population is to be found mainly in east coast Colon and west coast Panama City. It seems that crime is relatively limited among the *mestizo* populations of Panama, Costa Rica and Nicaragua. The incidence rises among the black or mulatto populations of all three. In fairness, it has to be said that these are also the poorest people in each country, with the relative affluence of the Panamanians mainly limited to the sizeable mestizo population. (There are few purebred Spanish families left in Central America.)

The final verdict on Panama? Though I wish it were otherwise, it has to be thumbs down. Especially after my travelling companion had his wooden crucifix, his most treasured possession, stolen from a rented room we were staying in.

CHAPTER THREE
NORTH AMERICA

USA

New York City

I have a love/hate relationship with New York. I love the buzz, the shops, the fact that you can walk most places in Manhattan, the restaurants, the feeling of a place that is still humming well into the night. On the other hand, I hate the rudeness of the cab drivers and shop assistants. The weather is too hot in summer and icily cold most of the winter, though of the two, I prefer the winter. But New York is best visited in spring or autumn.

I don't like Wall Street, but I do like the redeveloped Lower East Side around Washington Square, and the street atmosphere of Greenwich Village, SoHo, Tribeca and Riverside Drive. Central Park has its moments and the Metropolitan Museum is the best of its kind in the world. I have tramped miles up and down Fifth Avenue and Madison Avenue in particular. On the other hand, I don't have much to say in favour of Broadway, Times Square or 42nd Street, even if the area has cleaned up its act. As far as theatre districts go, I prefer London's.

I have never been to Staaten Island or the top of the Empire State Building or the Twin Towers. The New York I prefer is one of bookshops and small restaurants and delis serving up all kinds of goodies late at night, not to mention the Sunday edition of the New York Times after about 11 pm on a Saturday night. Once, when I was a member of the venerable Explorers Club, it also meant food and drinks by a blazing fire in winter and talks from members on their travels and adventures around the globe.

The worst thing about New York is the feeling that little counts there except money, and that all activity in life tends only towards that objective. This may be true in most large cities, but somehow the feeling is stronger in

New York than anywhere else on the planet. It's a feeling of ruthlessness at work in the interests of the individual, at the expense of the rest of us. For that reason, New York attracts young businessmen and bankers from far afield, keen to serve their apprenticeship in the school of hard knocks.

Los Angeles

Here is a city that I genuinely dislike. It wasn't always that bad. While LA was built around the car, at least the traffic used to flow 20 years ago. That is no longer the case. The smog is worse than ever and traffic often reduced to a crawl or a standstill. The last time I was in Los Angeles, the only place I could bring myself to go was the old Getty Museum on the Pacific Coast Highway. I haven't been to the new one, but from what I've heard, for all its size and opulence, it probably lacks the discreet charm of its predecessor.

Los Angeles to San Francisco

While Los Angeles is a city blighted by traffic and sprawling suburbs stretching mile upon flat and boring mile, it is the hopping-off place for the drive north via the coast to San Francisco. (Never take the inland freeway instead, unless you are in a hurry.) Malibu, the first point of note, is best passed without stopping. It's really only further north, after San Luis Obispo, that the coast gets interesting. From here it's not far to Hearst Castle. If you can forgive the lapse of taste in mixing centuries of European art and design in a single edifice, Randolph Hearst's ostentatious castle is worth a stop.

From here north the coastal highway ribbons mile after spectacular mile high along the cliffs to Big Sur, site of the Esalen Institute, the Big Sur Inn and Nepenthe,

the once famous cliffside home of Kim Novak, and now a restaurant.

There are three more places worth visiting between here and San Francisco. The first is Carmel, once an artists' village and now a town filled with endless pseudo-art and health-food shops. Despite the tourists who visit here by the coachload, the pretty town and prettier coastline are worth a day's stop.

The second place is Monterey, made famous by John Steinbeck's novel *Cannery Row*. This is a fishing port turned into a tasteful spot for visitors, and the seafood is as good and plentiful as ever.

And then there is Santa Cruz, another fishing town, with less charm than Monterey, but again worth visiting. This is where the Clint Eastwood horror story *Play Misty For Me* was filmed - no surprise, given that Eastwood lives in nearby Carmel where he was once the mayor.

Los Angeles to San Diego

For some reason I have always thought of Orange County as Richard Nixon country. The former President came from this ultra-Republican southern part of Los Angeles and eventually retired to it at San Clemente. The Southern California coastline down to San Diego is relatively built up most of the way. The better bits tend to be places like Laguna and La Jolla, though these coastal towns have lost much of their old charm thanks to overdevelopment.

San Diego itself is a much pleasanter city than Los Angeles, famous for its zoo and its sailing, but avoid its Ocean Beach on a hot summer day if you don't like wall-to-wall crowds. San Diego is the last city going south as you head for the Mexican border at Tijuana, the town where California fathers used to take their sons in the Fifties for their sexual initiation in one of the town's many bordellos.

San Francisco

San Francisco has grown too big for its own good. It runs into Oakland, which runs into Berkeley and so on. In the end it's all one big city as far as the visitor is concerned. But at least San Francisco has a discernible downtown that you can walk around, which is more than can be said for Los Angeles. San Francisco caters for the tourist big time, whether around the seafront shopping area of Ghirardelli or over the Golden Gate Bridge in Sausalito, once a sleepy fishing village that woke up to money and tourists following its discovery by the hippie counterculture in the Sixties.

I have a soft spot for Berkeley, having spent several weeks there during its student revolutionary period in the late Sixties. What is there today is a tame reflection of those times, when panhandling hippies covered the sidewalks. But as a student town centred on a famous university, Berkeley has its moments, not to mention good cafes, bookshops and cinemas.

Mendocino

You can get to this quiet town far north of San Francisco by driving over the Golden Gate Bridge and up the coast on Highway 1, or by going off course inland via Napa. The town of Napa has little to recommend to visitors, so unless you visit vineyards, the coastal route is more attractive and will take you, within 40 miles of San Francisco, to oyster-producing villages where small cafes serve up chowder to die for - and at prices that seem unbelievably cheap by European standards. One in particular that is worth a stop is Bodega Bay.

But drive the 80-odd miles north to Mendocino, a township that was once synonymous with the birth of the counterculture even before Haight Ashbury became a household name in 1967. Some argue that the hippie movement actually had its roots here. Others favour the theory that it developed out of the Monterey jazz festivals, the beat poets and prose writers like Jack Kerouac. Either way, the hippie legacy lingers on in Mendocino in bookshops and cafes that still reflect the heyday of the counterculture in a less commercial way than, say, Sausalito. The coast here is windswept and spectacular, the water freezing cold, even in summer. Best to go in spring or late summer. The air is always balmy, freshened by the ubiquitous giant sequoias of northern California.

Mendocino is where I set part of my novel, Black Jenny.

Columbus, Ohio

The epitome of suburban, middle America. Prosperous, Germanic and infinitely boring. Also unbearably hot in summer, necessitating a car to go anywhere and air conditioning to stay alive. I was once stopped by the police here for walking along the road in the middle of the day. Evidently, not being in a car made me suspect.

Indianapolis, Indiana

Even more boring than Columbus. Flat and predictable. You cannot get more Middle America than this. I flew in from New York and flew back the next day, unable to face more than 24 hours in the place. Too parochially depressing for words.

Detroit, Illinois

I drove through here en route from Columbus to Chicago. Fortunately I didn't stop.

Cambridge, Massachusetts

Home to Harvard University, Cambridge is a pretty town with a wide central area called Harvard Square. This is a public square, not to be confused with the equally pretty Harvard Yard. Here all of life seems to pass by, from Out-of-Town News and Tickets on Nini's Corner, to Brattle Street, which begins here and winds its way through the oldest part of the town, lined with houses going back to the seventeenth and eighteenth centuries in traditional New England architecture. Among them is Elmwood, the home of Harvard University's President. Cambridge is a small university town best visited in winter, in my opinion, when it's cold but the snow everywhere gives real atmosphere to the place. A short drive along the Charles River from Cambridge is MIT, a much less interesting institution than Harvard to look at. And a little further on still you come to Boston, a city that is too big and in most places too dirty for my liking, though I am sure the old town must be picturesque.

Another substantial part of my novel Black Jenny is set around Harvard.

Miami

It is probably true that Miami is the biggest Latin American city of them all. It also has some of the most expensive taxis in the world, as I recall from a $20 fare to travel from one end of the airport's runway to the other. Miami is everything that I hate about America, though I admit the airport has improved. It once took me over 12 hours to get through Customs there, having arrived with wife and two small children on Christmas Eve. Thousands of latinos arriving in front of me from Central and South America queued to get through, each searched from top to bottom in the hunt for drugs. Now you seem to be able to get through reasonably quickly.

The coast of Florida is condominiums, mile after mile of them, blocking the way to the beach for Joe Public. Most of the time you cannot even see the sea. Miami Beach is a high-rise nightmare that stretches all the way north to Fort Lauderdale and beyond. Palm Beach is little better - the sort of place where you can get arrested on suspicion of being poor.

The *lingua franca* everywhere is Spanish, though English is sometimes understood. Crime is a problem and for a time muggings of tourists used to be a daily occurrence. The bottom line is that Miami is best avoided unless you need to pass through its hub airport en route to somewhere else, usually Latin America or the Caribbean.

CANADA

Vancouver and the Rockies

I liked Vancouver, perhaps because there was an old friend there to show me round (which always helps to create a better impression). The city is modern, clean and seemed safe, the only dodgy bit being the druggy area on the fringes of Chinatown. The central shopping district of Vancouver is a cosmopolitan mix of locals and visitors, at least in summer. The climate at that time of year is warm and pleasant. And prices for a British visitor are affordable, thanks to the weakness of the Canadian dollar following the Pacific rim economic debacle. The city that Vancouver can best be compared with is Sydney. Both have a lot going for them at the moment. Sydney has more in the way of beaches, though as far as harbours go, I would say that Vancouver has the edge for spectacle, even without a harbour bridge and an opera house.

One of the best features of Vancouver is its seafood,

and there are plenty of outdoor places to eat at reasonable prices. If you do, order a well-chilled bottle of the best local Riesling that you can find and I guarantee that you won't be disappointed. It will come from one of the vineyards just west of the Rockies.

It's easy to drive in Vancouver and easy to park and find your way around. I have not been there in winter, but the skiing 30 minutes away across the harbour is said to be good, and Whistler, with some of the best skiing in North America, is only a short drive away, making weekend skiing a comfortable possibility.

The Canadian Rockies are quite unlike the Alps in Europe. They're not as high, but they are just as spectacular in their own way, thanks to their waterfalls and mineral-tinted lakes.

The townships of Jasper, Banff and Lake Louise are best visited in late summer when the crowds have left. Then they are pleasant places to stroll and shop. All have polite and helpful tourist offices, manned by young staff eager to answer questions about walking the many (well kept) trails in the Rockies.

The most interesting of these are often the least frequented - miles of broad, pine-needled tracks to lakes and waterfalls. The best are those following a ring path, so that you come back to where you started without covering the same ground twice.

Of the three townships, Banff is the largest, but Jasper probably wins on charm. Here elk still sometimes wander into town.

Take a walk to the far end of the lake at Lake Louise. It will take about half an hour each way and is an easy stroll for those not much into walking.

Toronto

I've been to Toronto twice, but never spent a night there. I can say that the feel of the place is like a cross between American and English. The architecture is distinctly American. But the manner of the people and feeling of relative safety is like a coming home for anyone British flying in from, say, New York. However, if I had to choose between several days in Vancouver or several in Toronto, I would opt for Vancouver any day. Toronto is the business hub of Canada, but if you're not on business, I cannot see much point in going there, except as a jumping-off point for other parts of eastern Canada.

CHAPTER FOUR
ASIA

SRI LANKA

This is the tourist destination that never quite happened, thanks to the tragic civil war that has endured in Sri Lanka since the early Eighties and has cost thousands of Sinhalese and Tamil lives. It's interesting to look at the way the hopes of countries are sometimes pinned on tourist revenues, only to see expectations dashed by events. It happened in the Seychelles with a left-wing coup just as tourism was taking off, then in Sri Lanka with the war of the Tamil Tigers for independence, and more recently in Egypt with fundamentalist attacks on tourists. Egypt is still reeling from millions of lost dollars.

I've been to Sri Lanka three times, in 1966, 1980 and 1999. Each time I've found a very different place, but the fact that I've gone back at all says I liked it. There aren't many places I visit three times.

In 1966 Colombo was typically post-colonial. There was a feeling of order and Britishness about the place. Some of that lingered in 1980, but by 1999 it was all gone. Sri Lanka is still an interesting place to visit, so long as you get out of Colombo. It's a mess and when it rains, it's worse. The streets are run-down and the buildings decrepit, despite some ostentatious high-rise hotels and office blocks that do nothing for the city's skyline. For all that, the terrible poverty that I saw on previous visits has diminished. But the war has taken its toll economically. My advice is to get out of town as fast as possible.

In 1980 the south-west coast of Sri Lanka was a laid-back stretch of beach, mile after mile, and south of the dreaded Hikkaduwa (Sri Lanka's answer to Goa) it really was enjoyable. Nice beaches and few hassles. All that has now changed, however. Hikkaduwa is a tawdry strip of about a mile lined with eateries, souvenir shops and cheap hotels all called 'Coral' something, though the only coral you'll find in the sea there is long since dead, killed by leaking fuel from the engines of the glass-bottomed boats. Be warned. Hikkaduwa is not for the beach lover who likes to get away from it all. Fortunately for the economy, local tourists now out-number the package holiday-makers for whom Sri Lanka and Hikkaduwa are synonymous.

Further south, beyond Galle, the ancient capital, there are still pretty stretches of beach, but here too the isola-tion has gone, as weekend villas and small hotels have sprung up. The foreign tourism that Sri Lanka has lost, thanks to the troubles, has been replaced, especially along this coast, by local tourism - sign of a rising lower-middle class that is everywhere in evidence.

But go to the tourist sites of the interior of Sri Lanka and you will be hard pushed to find other Westerners. Take Adam's Peak for example, a holy mountain once climbed by Marco Polo. You'll be lucky to climb its 2,000 steps in under two hours - if you can you're fit. The thousands of locals you'll encounter going up and down do it in groups of family and friends and make a day of it, eating and drinking along the way. If you're not a pil-grim, there isn't much to see at the top, except the Buddha's footprint, which is so big he must have stood at least 20 feet tall in his stocking feet. The view is said to be spectacular - all the way to the coast about 80 miles away - but all I saw was clouds. Still, worth it for the aer-obic work-out.

A drive along the high, narrow roads of the tea-grow-ing district in the centre of Sri Lanka, with its old British associations, is relaxing and colourful. There are a few spectacular waterfalls and the people are all friendly. In fact, the best thing about Sri Lanka is that outside Colombo it isn't difficult to engage friendly locals in conversation, generally without being hassled. People are only too eager to practise their English. One town that isn't worth the visit, though, is Nuwara Eliya, the centre of the mountainous tea district. It still shows off its English-style middle-class Victorian villas, built by the British planters. Most were shoddy travesties of English originals to begin with, and today are even shoddier hotels. The prices, though, are cheap.

However, there is a big plus side to the new Sri Lanka, and that is the east coast, as yet undiscovered except by the few Western surfers who stay (often for as little as £1.50 per night) in the cheap bungalows along the beautiful stretch of Arugam Bay, once a part of the off-limits Tamil territory, but now safe to reach if you don't mind half a dozen friendly army checkpoints along the way - and the chance to spot wild elephants in the grasslands a few miles out of town. Arugam Bay is blighted only by a small fetid lagoon at one end of the beach, and much of the fishing village's sewage seems to end up here. The villagers are still friendly, but it won't last, as their little corner of paradise gets discovered and eventually the bigger hotels move in. Meanwhile the place to stay, if you can afford about £12 per night for an immaculate bungalow and £3 per meal, is the Stardust, at the north end of the beach. Run by a Danish couple who have survived the Tamil troubles, it has to be the best value for money in food and accommodation in Sri Lanka. The seafood, all fresh, is to die for.

The Yala National Park lies about 40 miles to the south of Arugam. There is one tourist hotel at the park entrance, and while the food leaves a lot to be desired, the rooms are good. This is the place to be if you are interested in wildlife - bears, leopards, boar, crocodiles, eagles, deer, elephant, buffalo. Stay a couple of days and you'll see most of these, though you may have to rise at dawn to catch the leopards and the bears may not be too much in evidence. You cannot stay in the park overnight. You must be driven round by a guide, and you cannot get out of your vehicle except at a few spots, including two wild and beautiful beaches where it's possible to have a picnic and a swim.

For my money, a fourth visit to Sri Lanka would only

be worthwhile to spend more time in the national parks area around Yala and maybe visit Arugam again. In the interior, I would recommend a day's driving around the villages and hills of the tea plantation district. And if I go back, it will be when the Tamil problems are over and I can get to the coast around Batticaloa and Trincomalee. It's this eastern coastline that will one day become the real jewel in the crown for visitors.

Kandy, in the centre of Sri Lanka, is well worth a day's visit, though I prefer the market to the temples. If you don't mind the stench of the open sewers, it's one of the most interesting small markets I've seen anywhere.

INDIA

I'm not an India fan. I'll admit that here and now. Nor have I seen enough of India to be qualified to judge.

I've only had bad 'Delhi belly' twice in my life, and one of those times was in Delhi. (The other was in Morocco.) It's a city that's a dream for souvenir hunters. However, I hate to buy souvenirs and artefacts. Maybe I should be doing more to help local artisans, but I like to travel light and the thought of all that extra luggage (and excess baggage charges) does nothing to excite me. However, in Delhi you can visit the State Government Emporiums on Baba Kharak Singh Marg. Here it's possible to find, all in a row, shops representing every province in India and selling their local handicrafts at reasonable prices. Some of the provinces, such as Nagaland, ethnically a part of Burma, cannot be visited anyway.

Most visitors to India head for Agra to see the Taj Mahal for themselves. It always seems a bit odd, going to a place you know already from seeing it in a thousand photographs. The Taj Mahal lives up to expectations, though if you're like me, the first thing that will strike you on getting close is that the white marble is not as white or as smooth as you might have expected. The same can be said of the famous mosaic along the seafront at Copacabana Beach in Rio. It looks a lot cleaner and whiter in the photos.

I'm a Philistine when it comes to mogul palaces and temples - or any oriental palaces and temples for that matter, much preferring the European equivalent - so aside from the Taj Mahal, the other sites of Agra, the Red Fort and so on, didn't do a lot for me.

I preferred the next stop on the tourist circuit, Varanasi, where it pays to arrive before dawn to avoid the heat and crowds of fellow visitors. The only disadvantage in arriving so early is that if you are the first visitor, you will have a pack of dozens of beggars all to yourself - an unnerving experience, however charitable you might be feeling about poverty in the developing world.

The only way to see Varanasi is from a boat, of which there are many on offer. My lasting memories of the place are not so much the dilapidated old palaces of the maharajahs as the sight of bodies being burnt on the riverbanks, and of pilgrims brushing their teeth with finger or stick in the dubious waters of the holy Ganges, into which other pilgrims were busy emptying bowel and bladder. India, it is always said, is an assault on the senses, and nowhere is this more so than in Varanasi. Even the streets of Calcutta's poorest quarters do not compare.

Madras is a bustling Indian city and the jumping-off point for a mad dash by manic taxi to Mahabalipuram - one of the biggest tourist disappointments of all time. The famous temple on the beach is tiny and the monks posing as guides are so demanding that you half expect to be knifed if you don't cough up. I came away with a lasting dislike of Indian taxi drivers and their lack of regard for the people on the street, through whom they plough with scant consideration.

I took my six-year-old son round some of the poorest

parts of Calcutta so that he might learn how much poverty and suffering there is in the developing world and reflect on the relative privilege of living in a so-called developed country. It was a sobering experience for both of us.

Andaman Islands

We Brits tend to call them the Andaman Islands, as we still say Burma, and for a long time still said Ceylon and Rhodesia. We don't much like former colonies renaming places, though why the hell shouldn't they if it gives a sense of pride and national identity? The Indians call these islands simply Andaman. They are the more reachable part of Andaman and Nicobar. The latter group is technically off-limits to foreigners (and even to most Indians), ostensibly to protect the local tribes, though I've heard dark rumours that it has got more to do with the Indian naval base and allegedly nuclear weapons.

Well, I admit I would like to visit the Nicobars, and on my next visit to Andaman I hope to persuade the relevant official in Port Blair to authorise my passage on the ferry that takes a few hours to cross the Ten Degree Channel that separates Andaman from Nicobar.

Andaman is a large group of islands and the two types of visa that a foreign visitor can get will not allow you to go more than about 30 miles from Port Blair, the capital, though the islands themselves stretch about 100 miles from north to south. The people in Port Blair are almost all Indians, many from the mainland, and visitors are unlikely to see any of the tribal peoples who inhabit the forested regions to the north. The town itself is slow-moving, still quite colonial in feel, and there are few hassles as far as the visitor is concerned. Having said that, there isn't a lot to do there except visit the museum and the Round Prison, now a symbol of Indian independence from the yoke of British imperial power.

There are no good beaches near Port Blair, but if you can charter a boat for day visits or longer, there are islands within a couple of hours where the diving is still unspoilt, provided you pick a time of year when the water is clear and you like sharks. Andaman has a lot of sharks, and they tend to be of the serious variety - tigers and bull sharks, two of the three species most commonly implicated in fatal attacks (the white shark being the third). Don't venture near North Sentinel Island, though. It's still inhabited by a group of tribals with no contact with the outside world. They speared the last white man who tried to land on their island.

I'll go back to Andaman, for the diving and to try and get to Nicobar. It's only about two or three hundred miles in a straight line east from Port Blair to tourist-infested Phuket in Thailand, but the two places are worlds apart in every other respect.

The Indian people of Port Blair are friendly to outsiders, the cost of living is not much more than on the Indian mainland, and provided you don't mind the restrictions on travel, this place is worth a visit.

You'll have to swallow hard, though, when you see what they're doing to the rainforest here. Logging is big business in Andaman.

NEPAL

It has to be said that Nepal has passed its best. Not only are the political problems getting worse, but so is Westernisation, at least in Kathmandu.

There's much to see in the capital if you like temples and the like, but most visitors are in Nepal to go trekking or visit the Terai, the lowland area made famous by Tiger Tops, the ultra-expensive luxury lodge from which rich tourists set out to view rhinoceros on elephant-back. (They are unlikely to see a tiger, now that baiting with live goats has ceased.) The people of Nepal continue to be poor, and friendly to visitors along the trekking routes. Some of the money must be rubbing off, as they are not as poor as they once were.

The scenery is spectacular. It's always a thrill to see Everest, even if you went up too quickly, like I did (in a plane to 12,000 feet), and suffer as a result from altitude sickness, an unpleasant combination of headache and nausea.

Be prepared, too, for hot days followed by unimaginably cold nights as the temperature plummets.

I don't know how it is now, but when I left Kathmandu, the airport had the best airport restaurant I had found anywhere in the world - delicious local food at reasonable prices. Maybe that had something to do with the fact that the catering contract had gone to the Yak And Yeti, one of the best hotels in town.

INDONESIA

Bali

A n English travel writer once wrote that there was no point in going to Bali since it was already overrun with tourists. That was in the mid-Thirties. I didn't go there for the first time until the mid-Seventies. At that time there was one hotel at Kuta Beach, and a handful of *losmen* (cheap lodgings). The place was pleasant and friendly and inexpensive.

My second visit in the mid-Eighties left me feeling that Bali really was ruined this time, at least in the south, but that the north was still a pleasant place to go. However, I haven't been back to Bali since the late Eighties, and to be frank, there are better bits of Indonesia to see, further afield. After all, who wants to go to a place where it has become customary for Hindu families to charge tourists to witness the funeral of dead relatives, however much they may need the extra money to pay for the send-off?

You can even see funerals advertised on a big sign by the road as you approach Sanur.

Java

It's a slow process driving a car in Java. It's not so much the terrible condition of the roads, as the people and oxen and carts you have to weave around. There's an art to it, and if you drive like the locals with your hand on the horn, you will usually survive. Jakarta is one of those cities that the less is said about the better. It's the only place I've been obliged to bribe a traffic policeman (though I came close in the Dominican Republic). And the rush hour traffic makes even Bangkok a bit of a gift.

But get out on the open road (if you don't count the people and carts and oxen) and Java is an easy place to travel with your own set of wheels. There are cheap *losmen* to stay in and cheap but good things to eat, especially on the coast - and the south coast of Java has the biggest tiger prawns in the world (we're talking two to a meal).

I stayed in the village of Pangandaran and spent my days surfing. The place is filled at weekends with locals on holiday, with open-air pop concerts, and a thriving local prostitution industry, all safely set up in a purpose-built building - single storey, earthen floors. Strictly aimed at the local market though, with prices to match.

Sumatra and Nias

I haven't been to Rangoon, but when I got to Medan, the capital of Sumatra, I imagined this is what Rangoon must have been like before the present dictatorship took over. Medan is a sleepy vaguely colonial town, a bit on the boring side, but a safe and easy place, if somewhat humid. Come to think of it, Singapore must have been a lot like this before the war. I flew from here to Gunung Sitoli on the north east coast of Nias, over-flying Lake Toba, still a watering hole on the old hippie trail.

Gunung Sitoli is a hell-hole of a port town with little to keep the visitor there. It was, however, the hopping-off point for the tiny ramshackle boat that took us, squatting on the empty floor, down the coast of Nias to Telukdalam in the south, some eight hours away. Nias is a large island off the west of Sumatra where the people were still cannibals well into this century. Our goal was Lugundi, just a motorcycle ride away from Telukdalam.

Near Lugundi, where surfers from all over the world congregate, there is still a model longhouse village in the traditional style, complete with a stone about six feet high, over which once-were-warriors will jump if you pay them enough. For a further donation you will be invited to visit the interior of one of the giant longhous-es. All this commercialism hasn't turned the heads of the locals. They still live in the traditional way in the village, their income supplemented by selling artefacts to visi-tors from cruise ships stopping nearby for a shore visit. In the port of Telukdalam, a few miles distant, the way of life is modern (if that's the word) Indonesian. It's sur-prising that the old tribal way and the new can co-exist so closely together. The cost of living is ridiculously cheap, so long as you are prepared to eat fresh tuna and stay off the Coca Cola. However, there's a nasty variety of malaria about, and something nastier still that took the life of the young German who arrived with my son and me on the ferry from Gunung Sitoli. He was dead within a week of arrival.

SINGAPORE

There isn't anywhere in South East Asia that's quite like modern Singapore. It's a city that owes its well-heeled present to the administration of that benevolent dictator, Lee Kwan Yew, whose successors are busily carrying on the process of making downtown Singapore one of the most up-to-the-minute city centres in the world.

I knew the old Singapore in the Sixties. There was Bugis Street, Change Alley and the old Raffles. Today I'm not sure if Bugis Street still exists, Change Alley is a shopping mall under a giant high rise, and Raffles has been so refurbished that all its old down-at-heel colonial charm has been replaced with chic shops and a slick money-will-buy-you-anything kind of service that doesn't come cheap and leaves you longing for the good old days. Even the Long Bar is not where it used to be. The new bar resembles it in nothing but name.

But there is a positive side to the new Singapore, so long as you don't go and stay in one of the new hotels up the end of Orchard Road, with its miles of shopping emporia, sterile and air-conditioned. Much more fun is the downtown area where the locals have lunch in vast eateries under car parks, and tourists and locals eat and drink at the sidewalk cafes along both sides of the lower end of Singapore's river.

It's strange to imagine a cafe culture in Singapore, but that is what has emerged with the new affluence. The customers for the cafes and shops are more locals than tourists, who seemed very thin on the ground when I was in Singapore recently. The river must be the most sanitised in Asia, being cleaned daily by special boats that sweep the surface for the last remaining scrap of debris. I don't much like the humidity of Singapore, but in the evening after about 7 pm, when it's getting less sticky, the locals come out and, along with the tourists, start filling up the bars and cafes on either side of the river for about half a mile. On the other hand, venture out in the morning before 11 o'clock, by which time most of the rest of Asia has done its work for the day, and you will find that the shops are just opening and the cafes beginning to brew the first coffee. Suddenly

Singapore has turned into a city of night owls - so much so that the people seem unable to stir themselves much before the middle of the morning.

The old Chinatown, or at least a few streets of it, was about to be pulled down to make way for modern Singapore about ten years ago. A bit like the Rocks area of Sydney, where old colonial buildings were saved from demolition and restored, the shophouses of Singapore's Chinatown are in the process of being saved. It has been carefully done, but the result is a bit antiseptic. Gone are the old open sewers. The smells of the streets, which are a part of most Asian towns, are missing in Singapore. The new Chinatown survives now as a much more pricey shopping venue than it was before, aimed almost entirely at tourists, whereas once it served the local Chinese.

So what's the verdict on the new Singapore? Difficult to say. It's very safe to wander round. In fact most parts of the city centre would probably be safe for a woman on her own at any time of the day or night. Singapore must be one of the few cities in the world where the streets are safer now than they were thirty years ago. The old hustlers have died or retired into opulence. The only touts left nowadays are Indians in one street off the river, promoting the virtues of their *satay* sticks off the back of their stalls, and even that's pretty tame compared with the hustlers and pimps of the old days down by the waterfront and along Change Alley. There are supermarkets that have more in common with the food halls of Harrods than the markets of Asia. The prices in Singapore shops went from being among the cheapest in the world in the Sixties to some of the most expensive in the Eighties. Thanks to the Asian economic crash of the late Nineties, prices are back down to manageable level again, though that still hasn't brought back the tourists.

My advice is to see Singapore at least once, and to spend about two nights there. If you like it hot and sticky, make that three nights.

Malaysia

It's amazing what a country can do with a well orchestrated advertising campaign. I remember the market in Kuala Lumpur as the dirtiest and smelliest in the world, and the country as a whole as extremely boring. Then along comes a sustained advertising campaign in the West and people are suddenly showing an interest in Malaysia. There are turtles laying eggs on beaches, Penang if you like that sort of thing, and so on. I drove up from Singapore once and toured all over the place and, well, it was one big yawn. The place was safe, the people were friendly and unintrusive, but when all's said and done, there just wasn't much to do if you weren't the temples kind of traveller. Even the sea didn't seem real to a surfer like me - no waves.

Thailand

Few countries can have screwed up more in the race to promote all kinds of tourism, in a greedy attempt to cash in on the Western dollar. The result is a mess. Not that tourists are responsible for the congested streets of Bangkok - that's a local problem. But the rest of the country has simply gone to the dogs. Phuket must have been a nice place once to spend a few days by the sea. I got there for the first and only time in the late Eighties and already most of it was over-developed and getting a bit rough at the edges. It's not just the overspill of prostitution from the capital and that ugly coastal strip known as Pattaya, but a general sense that every visitor is viewed as a chicken ready to be plucked, as the French say. Add the jet-scooters and the paragliders behind boats and you get the picture. If they now have tourists being towed around the sea on giant inflatable sausages, I won't be surprised.

Those who fled Phuket but still loved Thailand discovered the island of Samui, in the Gulf of Thailand, in the Eighties. When I visited there in 1988 on a yacht, I met the Englishman who had married a local and built the first tourist bungalows on the island. He had had enough by then, what with the arrival of the package tourist companies and the mass market. Meanwhile on the neighbouring island of Phangan a new kind of hippie trail was clearly alive and well, with a beach full of naked Europeans high on weed and mushrooms. If you've read the cult book *The Beach* you'll get a bit of a feel for what you might now miss if you go to Koh Phangan ten years too late.

I stayed about a day and then moved on to more remote Koh Tao, and the tiny islet off its northern end called Nang Yuan. I had managed to avoid the tourist hell-holes of Chiang Mai and Pattaya. This was the other extreme, provided you had a boat. Otherwise forget it, unless you had infinite time and patience. The islet of Nang Yuan is only about five acres in area. It had about 20 cheap bungalows to stay in and one cheap outdoor eatery by the beaches - there are three beaches and they all back on to each other, making this one of the prettiest spots to stay, as well as one of the cheapest, that I have ever seen. The snorkelling is good by Gulf of Thailand standards, though it doesn't compete on an international level. We stayed on the boat anchored off and went ashore to eat.

Nearby Koh Tao was largely the home of a fairly wild-looking breed of fisherman or pirate - it was hard to tell which. I haven't been back since then, but *The Beach* tells me that soon after my visit the hippies on Koh Phangan moved on to Koh Tao.

No doubt a few of them are still living (or dying) there, and the pretty islet is now covered by fat Germans vying for deckchairs.

If you must visit Bangkok at all, try not to breathe or the air may kill you. Seriously though, apart from the Grand Palace, the Temple of the Golden Buddha and surrounding temples, all in one handy complex covering several acres, there isn't a lot to see and do in Bangkok except visit the markets, though the Floating Market is over-rated and best given a miss.

Forget about the girlie bars too, unless you are into that sort of thing. Even a walk along Patpong and the rest of them is disappointing. The thing that puts you off Bangkok most is the traffic and the diesel fumes. Belated attempts are being made to do something about it with an overhead monorail being built, but with 6,000,000 cars on the roads, it looks like a case of too little too late. The contrast with organised Singapore, the city with the most efficient traffic control in the world, could not be more noticeable.

JAPAN

It used to be that you needed a mortgage to afford a trip to Japan, the yen was so strong against the pound. While it's still not cheap, it is now more affordable.

Tokyo is like no other place you have been to. It's the only place I've ever been where a young woman has come up to me in the street as I peered at a map and asked me, without any ulterior motive, in halting English, if she could help me. The streets are not only safe, they are spotlessly clean, and the cleanest place of all is the underground, with its eateries and food untainted by the sort of filth in the air that Londoners are accustomed to when they travel by tube.

Tokyo has the brightest night-time lights in the world if you visit the bars and restaurants of Rippongi and Shinjuku. But make sure to have a Japanese with you if you want to catch a taxi after midnight, or you'll be lucky to get one to stop. If one does, and you don't have a piece of paper with directions to your hotel in Japanese, you're likely to spend an expensive few hours circling the city.

Even the Japanese can have a problem explaining where they live to a local taxi driver.

If you're unlucky and find yourself in an earthquake, as I did in Tokyo, try not to panic. At least it wasn't the Big One which, like southern California, they've been awaiting for years. Just duck the air-conditioners falling into the street.

Take a trip to Kyoto for the day. As I've said before, I'm not really much into oriental palaces and temples, but the imperial palace at Kyoto is worth a visit. On the other hand, a trip to the city of Osaka doesn't have a lot to recommend it for sightseeing. It isn't as clean or as cosmopolitan as Tokyo, but still feels just as safe.

The best thing about Tokyo, if you like to eat Japanese, is that you can have lunch and pay less than you would for a Japanese meal at home. The secret is not to go to a restaurant in the normal way, but to find the restaurant floor of one of the big downtown department stores. You don't even have to be a customer. You choose from one of the many small specialist eateries, each with its wares displayed as plastic models outside, and simply point at the one you want to try.

It isn't free, but it's subsidised by the store to attract customers and the prices are very cheap, while the quality of the food is generally good. I stayed at the New Otani Hotel, and since Japanese restaurants tend to specialise in only one type of cuisine - *tempura*, *sushi*, *teriyaki*, etc - there were dozens of different restaurants to choose from all within the hotel. Not subsidised like the department store eateries, but roughly the same quality.

CHINA

I've only done the tourist circuit in mainland China - Peking, Xian and Shanghai. Of these, I felt that only Shanghai would be worth a second visit. Peking was boring and even the Great Wall didn't make much of an impression, though I can confirm that it is visible from an aeroplane at 35,000 feet, so it's probably true when they say that it's the only man-made structure on earth that's visible from the moon. The most noticeable queue I found in Tiananmen Square was the one for McDonald's, which competed for customers with the queue for Mao's mausoleum.

Xian has several temples, but they left me unmoved, as oriental temples tend to do. The terracotta warriors were more interesting, though I felt sorry for the hordes of souvenir-sellers waiting outside to catch the smaller hordes of tourists getting off and on their buses. It seemed that the competition was so keen that artefacts were being given away - and we're talking about a pound for a necklace made of real jade.

Shanghai was the real eye-opener, and the highlight was a visit to the legendary Peace Hotel, with its octo-genarian jazz band who have played in the bar there since the Thirties, barring the odd spell in jail during the Cultural Revolution. Shanghai begs comparison with Hong Kong and, for my money, Shanghai is more inter-esting and colourful. The streets are alive at night with street vendors selling food of every description. Try bar-bequed sparrows on a skewer for the experience, how-ever awful. I wouldn't rate the food in general in Shanghai - or anywhere in China for that matter, except in the dining hall of the foreign section of Peking University, where it's a cut above the rest. About the best thing you can say about eating out in China is that it's cheap. Although I'm sure there are plenty of excep-tions, to eat good Chinese in China these days, you still have to go to Hong Kong.

Hong Kong

There's not a lot I can say about Hong Kong except that its shopkeepers are some of the pushiest, rudest in the world (after New York, of course). On the other hand, if you like to eat Chinese, this is the best place in the world to eat out. I haven't been there since it returned to the mainland Chinese fold, but I've heard it said that the economic problems following this move, and the slowdown in the Far East generally, have made the shopkeepers a lot more congenial than they used to be. Their 'don't waste my time if you don't want to buy' attitude, that used to be a feature of the street traders, must have been toned down. All in all, I'd give Hong Kong a miss unless you're a total Chinese foodie.

PHILIPPINES

If, like me, you like tropical islands, the idea of thousands of islands is fairly daunting. So I settled for just one, Luzon, the main island in the Philippines, and travelled around looking for waves to surf with an American friend. We stayed away from the north-east of Luzon rather than risk getting involved in the civil strife going on up there. What we did see made little lasting impression. Manila is said to have the highest number of guns per private citizen of any city in the world, and a murder rate to match. The place didn't seem unduly dangerous to wander around at night, but that probably had more to do with the US military presence nearby than the law-abiding nature of Manila's citizens.

The Philippines don't rate touristically, except for a few well-publicised outlying islands, which is probably a blessing for travellers looking to escape from fellow Westerners. I can't see the Philippines taking off as a tourist destination, though. Maybe the whole security picture just doesn't inspire enough confidence. They no longer speak Spanish in the Philippines, but it's worth remembering that once this was a Spanish colony. The result is that there is still something of the feel you get travelling in a lot of Central America, never quite sure just how far you can let your guard down against crime.

CHAPTER FIVE
ATLANTIC

CANARY ISLANDS

Grand Canary

If you're like me, you don't like to stay too long in most places. The best thing about Grand Canary is not the town of Las Palmas, which long ago sold out to mass tourism, nor the beaches, since there aren't any except the windy stretch of Maspalomas in the south. The best thing is the spectacular drive along the cliffs of the south-western side of the island. As with so much of the Canaries group, the attraction lies in the ruggedly beautiful scenery.

Tenerife

Again the appeal of this Canary Island is in the scenery. The best time to visit is outside the hot summer period. Drive south through the central high country around the smouldering volcano of Teide, through cool ancient forests, then along the rugged southern strip to the west of Playa de las Americas, a god-forsaken spot on the coast thanks to the worst kind of tourist development. Also there are few real beaches except artificial ones, a fact of life in most of the Canary Islands.

However, this southern coastal area is the jumping-off point for Gomera, an island worth a visit if you like to tour around parts of Spain's seafaring past.

Gomera

It looks a small island on the map, but because the roads are long and winding, it takes hours to drive from one side of the island to the other. At the start is the church of San Sebastian, alleged to have been visited by

Christopher Columbus as he set out on his first voyage to the New World. When you get to the other side of the island, the only beach is Playa de Vueltas, a bleak black-sand beach. But the real pleasure of this island is just in the travelling, whether you drive or get out and walk. The scenery in the high centre, especially when the flowers are out in spring, is every bit as romantic as, say, pastoral Switzerland. And the best thing of all is that there aren't lots of other tourists.

Hierro

This is probably the least visited island in the Canaries. When I was there, the only place to stay was a pretty little lodge run by Germans for divers at Punta de la Restinga, the southern tip. Curiously, when we stayed the night there they were showing old German wartime newsreels on video. Everyone was very pleasant, but you couldn't help getting the feeling that the owner was maybe a refugee with a Nazi past.

Hierro is half of a volcano that has mostly slid into the sea. It has a tiny population and, if you're not into diving, there is little to do except walk among a few volcanic fumeroles that make you wonder if the ground will blow up at any moment. Or, if you are there in spring, you can walk among fields of wild flowers that carpet virtually the whole island as it slopes away from the airfield in the north down to the southern tip a couple of miles away. There are no beaches, but the Germans have a great spot for swimming off the rocks.

La Palma

This is the yachtsman's favourite island, and many boats heading across the Atlantic take off from here. If you ever saw a forgettable film called *The Land That Time Forgot* starring John Wayne's son, this is where it was filmed. The island has another volcanic crater, though less attractive than Gomera's and Hierro's. There are a few villas on the high slopes at the northern end of the island and any beauty in the island is at this end. But all in all, it's the least attractive island in the Canaries.

Lanzarote

This Canary has survived package holiday tourism remarkably well, despite having only one real sandy beach, Playa Blanca. Lanzarote is best known for its camel trips up a volcano and its underground grotto (surprisingly, worth a visit). It's a generally inviting island of stark landscapes and good restaurants at cheap prices. Probably worth a two-day visit, but you would have to like package holidays or be mad to go for two weeks. On the other hand, you can get a small ferry from the northern end to the small island of Graciosa.

Graciosa

This place is weird and beautiful. For one thing the entire population numbers about 50 inbred souls all living in Caleta del Sebo, a small fishing village where the ferry comes in. Don't expect them to talk to you if you go over there. You may get served in the only bar, but that's about as friendly as it gets. Here they really don't like outsiders, and that includes people from the mainland (meaning Lanzarote). I went with my surf-board and enough water to survive for a day. There are no vehicles for hire - I'm not even sure there are any vehicles. I followed a track across what seemed like desert to the far side of Graciosa about five miles away, and there went surfing, having lugged my board the whole way in the heat. This is about as far away from tourists as you could hope to get in the Canaries. I didn't see a living soul the whole way across and back. No real beaches, mind you - just rocky shoreline that would have been a dream for diving if I'd had the gear. When I got back to the bar on the other side, it was all I could do to persuade the surly local to serve a cold drink. Then it was on to the ferry and back to Lanzarote about three miles away. Don't expect to be able to spend the night in a place like this unless you camp, but for a bit of day adventure this was great.

Fuerteventura

This windy island, as its name suggests, has only climbed into the tourist brochures in the last 20 years. I can remember it before and I've seen it since. Fortunately, the mass-market tourism is concentrated around two or three townships, and as the island is big, it's possible to get away from it all without any trouble. A four-wheel drive vehicle, while not essential, is a great asset, especially if you drive the mean road around the northern end of the island, west of the tourist capital of Corralejo, or go to the far south and tackle the road to Jandia, one of the wildest-looking beaches on earth. Here the walk to the sea is a quarter of a mile across the sand, and on the cliffs is a gaunt ruin of a building said to have been built by the Nazis as a communications centre for their Atlantic submarine fleet.

Fuerteventura's other claim to fame is that the Spanish Foreign Legion used to be based here, but were kicked out in the Seventies after a few of them raped a tourist. After that, they were banished to nearby Spanish Sahara, now part of Morocco.

Off the north-east tip of the island is a small island called Lobos, a reference to the Atlantic monk seals that used to inhabit it centuries ago, and are now extinct except for a small group still to be found in Mauritania. Lobos is home to a surfer's dream - a long right-hander that breaks off the north-western end in winter. I discovered the spot in January 1977 and surfed it for the first time, having christened it Punta Chiquitas (short for Punta de las Olas Chiquitas - Cute Little waves) or Chiquitas for short. Its ancient Spanish name, according to maps, is Punta Salidero. The waves were a mean 12 foot the first day.

CAPE VERDE

Sal

This island comes first because it has the only international airport. Two airlines dominated here in the past - South African Airways and Aeroflot, which built a huge concrete monolith that claims to be a hotel. It went up in the days when Cape Verde was one of the USSR's client states. Today the run-down township of Santa Maria could be called the capital of Sal. The island has little to recommend it if you are not a surfer or windsurfer. Even a spell on the rather unattractive beach is an ordeal as the sand never seems to stop blowing in your face. This was the place where I first ate crocodile. No, there are no local crocodiles. It had been flown in from South Africa.

Maio

One of the least known of the Cape Verde islands, Maio is probably the most interesting. The only accommodation we could find was of the home-stay variety in the house of the local mayor. It was clean, comfortable and cheap. We rented a pick-up truck and toured the island. This one too was wind-blown, which was a pity, as there are more beaches on Maio than all the other islands in the group put together if you exclude Sal. The town centre has one small cafe, where it's possible to get the inevitable Cape Verde meal - grilled tuna with rice - all for next to nothing. Wash it down with a cold beer, with a tomato salad on the side and what more could you ask for after a day at the near-by beach, which stretches for miles in both directions, and you've got it all to yourself. The people in the Cape Verde Islands weren't very hospitable on the whole, but on Maio they were, perhaps because they were not in the habit of seeing Western visitors. When we approached one village in the north of Maio, the entire populace came out to stare at us in disbelief when word of our arrival spread.

Santiago

Santiago is the most developed island in Cabo Verde. Here there is a cobbled road, the only one of its kind in the world to have been built by convicts and still in use today. It must have taken years as there are some 50 miles or more of it. It meanders through an island that has most of the vegetation in Cabo Verde, and while few people look remotely affluent among the half-cast population of this volcanic island group, a few in Praia, the capital, look vaguely comfortable and own the odd beaten-up old car or two. For a visitor like me, though, there wasn't a lot to see or do. Praia has a market where the feeling is not particularly good. This is, after all, one of the poorest countries in the world, one in which 80 per cent of GDP is in the form of aid. I spent most of my time in Praia in the local airline office trying to confirm my flights around the archipelago.

Getting my surfboard on the small local planes was a nightmare, as it often is. Usually they have never seen a surfboard before. Then there is the language problem (we're talking pidgin Portuguese here). Then there is the problem of fitting a surfboard into a pint pot of a luggage hold, while avoiding excess luggage charges. Just reconfirming local flights on an airline that changed its schedules from one day to the next was a battle in itself. As Praia is the hub airport for flights around this island group, we got to know Praia's airport quite well in the course of our stay.

Boa Vista

As its name suggests, this island is fairly nice-looking in a rugged, empty, wind-swept kind of way. However, that's where its charm ends, unless you happen to be a world-class windsurfer, as this is where they come to try and break the world speed record, taking advantage of the steady high winds that blow all the time across the island.

There's one reasonably modern small hotel, which is saying something for Cabo Verde. It's on the edge of the only township, a dusty place with the feel of one of those Western movie towns like Tombstone, Arizona. And the locals are definitely not friendly here. Maybe it's because the windsurfers have given the island its first taste of tourism and that has been sufficient to ensure alienation.

However, there are spectacular and lonely walks for miles along the coast, with huge sand dunes and beach of a sort in one direction, and rocky cliffs and rockier sea in the other as far as you care to go - and not another human being in sight.

Fogo

The Portuguese seem to have liked to keep things creative when it came to naming islands. Either you picked a name that described the place - Fogo for a volcano, Sal for a salt pan island, Praia for a beach - or you gave it the name of the saint on whose day it was discovered - for example Sao Vicente. Failing further inspiration, you could always try the month in which you got there - hence Maio.

Fogo is a god-forsaken place of dried and barren lava round most of the island, with a coastal strip of vegetation around the rest. If you get the urge to dive here, pick a time of the year when the water is clear. It often isn't, and you would not want to be taken by surprise by sharks that saw you before you saw them.

Jacques Cousteau dived in these islands and pronounced them to have the highest density of tiger sharks in the world. I would bestow that honour on the Andaman Islands myself, but then again, it's only my word against Captain Cousteau's.

The one small hotel in the one small township has the only swimming pool that I'm aware of in Cabo Verde. The bad news is that it has no water in it and has been that way for years.

The worse news is that you could get stuck on Fogo, as the airline has a habit of overbooking and locals get automatic priority over tourists, even if you have an onward international flight to catch from Sal. So checking in at the piece of corrugated iron that passes for an airport terminal on a rocky shoreline can be a bit of a cliffhanger. Don't despair if you miss the flight. Try to find someone with a fishing boat and bribe them to take you to Brava, the tiny furthest island in the archipelago, about ten miles further on. I haven't been there, but it looks enticing from high on the coast road round Fogo, and better still, it's said to have more tiger sharks than the other islands.

There are three other inhabited islands in Cabo Verde - Santo Antao, Sao Vicente and Sao Nicolau. I hope to go back one of these days and visit them, along with Brava. Would I go back to any of the five I have already been to? The answer is 'yes' to Sal, for the surf, but a hesitant 'no' to the other four. Praia is the only island with considerable vegetation and has the most history, but it's also the most populated by far. If I had to invest in the future of one of the islands for carefully controlled tourist development, it would be Maio - but we're talking 50 years from now, and assuming that by then it would have an international airport of its own. It will happen one day, and Cabo Verde will develop, if that's the word, along the lines of the Canaries. The wind will be a drawback, but it hasn't put people off Fuerteventura, so why should it put people off Sal and Maio and Boa Vista and the rest?

MADEIRA

I can't claim to have known Madeira in the old days, having only gone there for the first time in the mid-Nineties. However, it wasn't difficult to see how it might have been once. It must have been really nice and a great place to drop in on for a bit of winter sun. However, the sad fact is that Funchal and the surrounding area has been horribly overdeveloped. You can smell local greed and corruption in the air. A town the size of Funchal shouldn't need ring roads and overpasses and under-passes for traffic, and until a few years ago it didn't. Now there are too many hotels, too many cars and too many people. As for the buses that lumber round blind corners on some of the narrowest and most dangerous roads in the world - one can only wonder at the fact that the accident figures are not even higher than they are.

All of which is a pity. The mighty Reid's hotel is still there - clinging to the cliffside and to its elegant past despite the surrounding onslaught. The rules are still strict there - jacket and tie for dinner, and so on. But like Raffles in Singapore, Reid's is a bit of a parody of its former self. The clients have more money than breeding these days and what's left of the old gentry who once went there have moved on to more private haunts not yet discovered by brash new money.

Almost all foreign tourism in Madeira is restricted to

the area round Funchal and the airport, so if you're prepared to venture around the coast there are villages in
the far west where visitors are a rarity and still treated
with a certain degree of suspicion.

If you were to go to Madeira at all, I would suggest
you go in autumn or spring and stay in the far west, say
in the coastal village of Jardim do Mar with its sea-swept
scenery. There is one small restaurant with a couple of
rooms to rent.

Porto Santo

Three days in Madeira is probably enough, and in any
case there's a lot more peace and charm on nearby
Porto Santo, the island where Christopher Columbus
married the local governor's daughter. The small governor's house is now a museum. Vila Baleira, the only village, is very small and surprisingly friendly. And a
rental car will take you round the island in a few hours.
The atmosphere reminded me of the island of Graciosa
in the Azores. The few hotels in Porto Santo aren't much
to write home about, and frankly one of the small guesthouses in the town is a lot more fun. There's a long
empty beach that you'll see in the brochures, but it's not
really the place for an enjoyable swim. If you're like me,
you'll prefer to swim off the rocks somewhere along the
other side of the island.

AZORES

The Azores are like the Canaries used to be - in other
words, few tourists, though there are quite a lot of
mainland Portuguese who arrive in the summer.

These islands are well spread out and the big differ-
ences between them reflect their very separate development in past centuries, when transport was not easy and
meant a long sailing journey from island to island.

99

Sao Miguel

The largest island in the Azores, Sao Miguel and its capital Ponta Delgada have benefited enormously from development funds from the EU. When I first went there, the place was pretty poor. The second time, it was actually quite prosperous. San Miguel is best seen in the spring, when its fields, and those of the other islands in the Azores, are carpeted in flowers. Failing that, autumn is the best time to visit, though in summer it's not as warm as, say, the Canaries further south.

Sao Miguel is known for its picturesque lakes (Sete Cidades) in the west and its thermal spa area (Furnas) to the east of the island. Unlike the Canaries and Madeira, the Azores are very green (with a couple of exceptions) and Sao Miguel is the greenest of them all. On the other hand, there are not a lot of beaches, either here or on most of the other islands.

What beach there is on Sao Miguel is on the north side. But the coastline is attractive for all that and, for those willing to swim from rocks, there is no lack of small bays to spend the day at along the north coast. Just for a drive in beautiful surroundings, Sao Miguel is worthwhile, reminiscent of driving round Ireland's Ring of Kerry on a hot summer's day.

Santa Maria

This is one of those less verdant islands. It has an airport mainly because it was once a stopping point for trans-Atlantic flights, rather like Bermuda, in the days before planes where able to make it across the pond in a single jump. My first visit was in the small hours of the morning, flying Freddie Laker from Barbados to London in 1972. The next time around, I flew in as part of a circle flight around the Azores and stopped for a couple of days. I was the first tourist the island had had for ages and they were so surprised that they put me on the local radio to find out why I had come. The answer was in fact simple: I had come to explore for surf. The ubiquitous Christopher Columbus popped up again when I got to the far side of the island. This time it was the small church where he had prayed before leaping into the unknown the following morning. After that it was straight into the surf to catch a few waves in the shadow of the church. And by the way, Santa Maria has the only genuinely white sand beach in the Azores and they're very proud of it.

Faial

Another fairly barren island, and one that receives very few visitors from abroad, though the small township of Horta and its harbour are charming. When it comes to yachtsmen, Faial is to the Azores what La Palma is to the Canaries. It's one of those last jumping-off spots before hitting Antigua or San Salvador or wherever, though obviously Columbus was unaware of this and went to the wrong island for final prayers. On the other hand, he knew to avoid the more touristy islands, his route taking him through Gomera in the Canaries then Santa Maria in the Azores.

Faial has a wind-swept bay, Praia do Norte, on one side, and I will always remember it for the fact that despite years of experience in treacherous surf, I had a close call here, bouncing off the rocks as I tried to find a safe way out of the water.

The first local surfer, Joao Carlos, showed me around the town and we had dinner together with the local mayor, who picked my brains for an hour about the best way to encourage tourists to Faial. He didn't seem to believe me when I suggested he say and do nothing, in order to keep the place a secret for the few who would ever find their way there.

Terceira

This is a strange island as there is a giant American military base here. However, it has very little contact with its surroundings, as I found out when I got invited there for Christmas dinner a few years ago. The base has cinemas, bowling alleys and its own radio station. Food, even milk, is flown in daily from the USA, even though cows are a feature of the local landscape. Having said that, the landscape is not much to write about, and frankly I wouldn't have gone to Terceira, not once but twice, had I not been hunting for surfing spots. Not that the surf was up to much either.

The locals, inevitably, seemed somewhat disaffected as a result of the proximity of thousands of US soldiers, and who could blame them, given that the Americans seemed to have little awareness of or interest in their surroundings, despite a cultural offensive by their radio station that amounted to a new Portuguese word being broadcast each day to try and get them to integrate a bit.

Graciosa

Graciosa is rarely visited by outsiders other than mainland Portuguese. For all that, it's one of the prettiest islands in the group, which probably explains its name. There's a rambling main township with a giant pond and a baker's shop that sells delicious bread if you can ever find it. And there's the usual fringing road around the perimeter of the island, with the odd coastal hamlet along the way and one or two places where you can even get a good seafood meal and a beer. Beaches are almost non-existent but there are plenty of good rocky spots for a swim.

Quite a friendly island as far as the Azores go, even walking around the central area near the pond in the evening with all the locals.

Pico

Pico is a barren island that is basically a single volcano. It is best reached by ferry from nearby Faial. The crossing is a dramatic one that passes strange rocks jutting out of the sea. The arrival, it must be admitted, is bleak, the village (Madalena) where you arrive looking woefully transient upon an expanse of volcanic scree and lava, as poor a place as you are likely to see in the Azores, unless EU money has tarted it up since I was there.

Sao Jorge

It would be nice to think that they named this island after England's patron saint. Well in a way they did. However, Saint George was no doubt patron to many others also, including a lot of Portuguese. It's a green pastoral island along its north side and very pretty in the spring. However, there are virtually no foreign visitors, so anyone non-Portuguese will be looked at curiously. Not that people are much in evidence. In fact, we hardly set eyes on a living soul. Again no beaches, although there were plenty of rocks to jump off into the sea.

Flores

Flores is about as far west as you can go in Europe. After that it's all ocean until you get to Bermuda and the Caribbean. It must have been a lonely part of Portugal for many centuries, cut off by about 100 miles even from the main Azores islands to the east. I found Flores charming. It lived up to its flowering name, as I came in spring and found hedges of hydrangeas everywhere, thousands of flowers in every direction on a green pastoral background. Though it looks tiny on a map, even here a rental car can be useful. A drive around goes through fields and woods and the odd hamlet. The coast is rugged and there are no beaches. But there are plenty of places where a swim off the rocks is feasible. And on the outskirts of the main town is a tidal swimming pool among the rocks, a common sight in much of the Azores, as well as Madeira.

I don't normally remember places to stay, but the one in the township on Flores stuck out for the friendliness of the woman who ran it and the cleanliness and attention to detail that are a feature of her guesthouse. The food, too, was excellent and the place is called Residencial Vila Flor.

Corvo

The smallest island in the Azores, this one is a short distance across the water (a couple of miles) from Flores and can only be reached by the once-a-day ferry. The island has one tiny harbour village and one house that does B and B. You could walk round the village in five minutes - and everyone on the island would be aware of your presence by then. There is only one - very short - road and it goes up the hill to the volcanic craters, now lakes, that form the centre of the island. However, if you are feeling strong, make the walk - it's about two miles - on foot. You will pass more hydrangea hedges and, if it's spring, the island will seem unreal, a sea of flowers on a sunny island floating somewhere far out in the Atlantic. The whole island cannot be more than about four miles across.

There isn't a lot going on in the port village, but you can always find a bar to engage the curiosity of the locals, and there is one place to eat. The seafood is guaranteed to be fresh in a place like this.

CHAPTER SIX
CARIBBEAN

BERMUDA

Bermuda isn't strictly part of the Caribbean. In Shakespeare's time it was known as the Isle of Devils. If only it were still that exciting. The trouble with Bermuda is that it's too organised. Fortunately, there was a bit of excitement when I was there - the worst hurricane in living memory. And since this was Bermuda and not Guatemala, fortunately there was little damage. Every house is required by law to be hurricane-proof, which means massive white- tiled roofs.

Tourists can't rent cars in Bermuda, which is how they try to keep the traffic under control. The locals are only allowed one car per household - that's per household, not per house. So they put several kitchens into a single dwelling in order to pretend they are several households, and that way they get to have more cars. The result is endless traffic that takes a lot of the joy out of cycling or motorbiking round the islands as a tourist. (There are several islands, but as they are linked by bridges, it may as well be a single island.)

There are a few pretty beaches, but the water is only warm in summer and autumn. Arrive in January and, though the air will be mild and pleasant, the water will be too cold for swimming. But the real problem is what to do in Bermuda. The rich expat community and the likes of former US presidential hopeful Ross Perot hide in palatial villas behind high walls. The local black population, while not so rich, is better off than blacks anywhere else in the New World. So if you know someone, you might be invited around and have a reasonable time for a few days. But know no one and you will die of boredom, if you don't first get killed being overtaken on your motorbike by a local driver on the narrow roads.

Some visitors settle for the much touted diving trips around the island, but frankly I'd rather head for the Turks and Caicos or the Bahamas if I wanted good diving in this corner of the globe. All food is extremely expensive, being mainly imported, even most of the fish. If you must go to Bermuda, spend only about four days there if you don't know anyone. Visit the beaches and museums. And don't walk on the roads. There are few pavements and an endless stream of cars zipping by inches away.

BAHAMAS

Cat Island

The Bahamas stretch a very long way, and each island group is quite different from the next. Provided you stay away from the ultra-touristy places like Grand Bahama and Nassau (New Providence), things can really get interesting. What I'm leading up to is the so-called Out Islands. Take Cat Island for example. There is one good place to stay not far from the airstrip. Rooms are thatched bungalows with ensuite outdoor showers screened by coconut matting walls. If you probe hard enough on Cat Island, you'll begin to find that voodoo and the black arts are still believed in and probably practised among some of the older people on the island. Don't go to Cat Island for beaches, though. The water is clear and the skin-diving good on the east coast if you like rough water, but this is not a beach kind of a place. Best way to get around is definitely a hired bike. Cat Island gets the thumbs up for a three-day visit. Even the locals are quite friendly, which is saying a lot for the Bahamas. Best inland visit is a hermit's cell high on a hill.

Long Island

Long Island is like a bigger version of Cat Island, and you'll find it easier to get around with a rental car here. Go to the southern tip and you'll find a fishing village where the daily cleaning of the catch brings lemon sharks right up to the water's edge. Go swimming here and you're almost guaranteed to find large rays under your nose in the shallow lagoon.

As with Cat Island, don't expect too many pretty beaches on Long Island. There are caves with bats to lure the visitor instead.

San Salvador

This place is so special for me that I shouldn't even be mentioning it. It's not for nothing that Club Med have set up here with a place devoted exclusively to diving. There isn't much else to do on San Salvador, except visit old ruined plantation houses.

But drive in a rental car to French Bay on the south shore of the island, near a former plantation called Watlings, and find a white sandy beach all to yourself (not difficult as you'll probably be the only visitor on the island apart from the Club Med lot, and they go everywhere by boat). The water in front of your white sandy beach looks like water anywhere in the tropics - warm and inviting. What you don't realise until you step in is that a few yards offshore are the most incredible coral gardens, in about five metres of water. I've seen the best of many tropical dive sites, including the Maldives, Fiji, the Turks and Caicos Islands, the Seychelles, the Tuamotus, to name a few, but for sheer underwater splendour, this took the prize - there was a forest of giant living elkhorn coral, there were turtles, sharks and fish aplenty. And all stretching towards the horizon from just a few yards off the beach.

On the other hand, if you don't like snorkelling or scuba diving, San Salvador hasn't got a lot to offer. I can't even say if the locals are friendly, as there are hardly any.

Eleuthera

Eleuthera is not an island I would go back to. I stayed at Cotton Bay, somewhere in the middle of this elongated island, and found this old and rich American enclave dead boring. I didn't get to Harbour Island in the north, which has the unusual distinction of having a larger white than black Bahamian population. Eleuthera is long and requires a car to get around. The sea is never far away on either side, and the snorkelling is good almost anywhere you care to stop. Locals are on the unfriendly side of indifferent, and basically Eleuthera gets the thumbs down.

Mayaguana

Most people have never heard of the last island in the Bahamas chain. It has two separate communities, Abraham's Town and Pirate's Well, each the descendants of slaves freed in Bermuda in the seventeenth century. The two villages don't speak to one another and most of the men are called the Reverend Something or Other. In other words they tend to be a bit on the inbred side and not a little crazy. For all that, I spent a great couple of days in Abraham's Town. I stayed in the house of a local woman who took lodgers, and one of her relatives turned out to have the only fuel and the only boat on Mayaguana. I bought the fuel and this entitled me to a trip in the boat to a vast lagoon about ten miles east of the settlement. There three of us spent two hours diving for conch in about five metres of water among fan corals and nurse sharks. We brought up about half a ton of conch - a thousand dollars worth, I was told, on Nassau's wholesale market. As we chugged back to the settlement, the skipper and his two crew extracted the conch and tossed the empty shells into the sea. I arrived back in the village fit from so much diving, satisfied that I had found one of the most unusual and beautiful places in the Caribbean. What could be better than to be among friendly locals, the only Westerner within 50 miles?

TURKS AND CAICOS

I've enjoyed this place so much that I've been three times and visited five of the islands in the group. My favourite is Grand Turk, for the charm of the Salt Raker Inn in town (it's actually only a village) and the fact that the Caicos Channel plunges to a depth of about two miles only 100 yards offshore from the small unhurried capital, the village of Cockburn Town. The diving off Grand Turk is good, but on South Caicos it's sensational, which is just as well as there isn't anything else much here. The whole island group was once a major drugs centre, South Caicos in particular. You would fly into the airport above a clutch of small aircraft wrecked in the shallow waters of the lagoon below. Either they were taking off or landing overloaded with dope, or the pilot was stoned - or both. The township of South Caicos is about as rough as it gets, so unless you are there for the diving, give it a miss.

Most tourists head for Providenciales, known to everyone as Provo. This is where all package tourism has been concentrated in recent years, with a heavy emphasis on the US market and on diving holidays. I don't particularly like the American way of travel with all that emphasis on resorts and (ultra-expensive) hide-aways. If you want to get the same beaches all to yourself in more simple surroundings, head for North Caicos and stay at the Ocean Beach Hotel, a small place where the food is good and the beach is all yours, miles and miles of it. You can swim across the lagoon out to the reef a mile offshore, sometimes accompanied by friendly barracuda in about three metres of water. And apart from that, there isn't much to do on the island except dance to bluebeat at the nearby Prospect of Whitby Hotel or cycle around and maybe visit the crab farm and the flamingo pond.

HAITI

Most travellers won't be going here, if only because it is not exactly the safest place to wander around if you happen to be white. I went at a time when it was a bit dodgy, and now it's reputedly even riskier. The capital, Port au Prince, is a bit of a hell-hole. The really interesting place to go is Cap Haitien in the north. There are a couple of small hotels where visitors can barricade themselves in. The streets are vaguely reminiscent of Louisiana and the pirate ride at Disneyland - all faded eighteenth-century French colonial architecture. In fact very faded, since there was little electricity when I was there and most places were lit at night with oil lamps and candles. This was the principal trading centre of the Caribbean in the mid-eighteenth century and the wealthiest town in the West Indies. To see such once glorious architecture now reduced to a shadow of its former self is an eerie thing. The poverty is intense and the traveller can be left feeling uncomfortable. Not only is the conscience pricked here like nowhere else, including India, but there is definitely a feeling of personal danger, especially wandering among the crowds watching voodoo rites in the streets on a Saturday night.

The beaches in northern Haiti are pretty, but the prettiest of all are along the southern shore of the island, as you move in the direction of the border with the Dominican Republic from the coastal township of Jacmel. Here too is aching poverty, and the traveller with a rental car, as I had, is best advised to take a tough local kid along as a guide if menacing looks and machetes are not to escalate into violence. I've been all over the eastern Caribbean, and this was the only place I've felt any real sense of danger. The one hotel in Jacmel was like a citadel in a sea of poverty. The coastline east of here, with its fishing hamlet of Marigot, is one of the most picturesque coastlines I have ever seen. Needless to say, there wasn't another European in sight, or any facilities for tourists apart from that one hotel.

DOMINICAN REPUBLIC

The island of Hispaniola is taken up two-thirds by the Dominican Republic and one third by Haiti. The capital Santo Domingo has a fascinating history, its first bishop being the brother of Christopher Columbus himself. Nowadays the place has a strong *mafioso* feel about it, in the style of much of Central America and Mexico in particular. Whenever film-makers in recent years have made a movie about pre-Castro Cuba, they have invariably filmed it in Santo Domingo. The capital has an air of Latin corruption and criminal opulence. I got stopped by a traffic cop on my first day and asked for a 'fine' for having a surfboard on the roof-rack of my car. He was fat and mean-looking with the standard pistol on his hip, but I managed to save my wallet by acting dumb and pretending not to understand Spanish.

I stayed one night (complimentary, thank God) at the incredibly expensive La Romana hotel, one of the few resorts in the world to have a private international airport for its guests, a golf course with several greens on offshore islands and a room service that arrives by golf cart. It's the sort of place that Frank Sinatra used to visit. I met the manager and learned that his son was the country's ambassador to Britain at that moment, and spent most of his time conducting business from Annabel's in Mayfair. I didn't ask what kind of business. The poverty outside the resort was in sickening contrast to the wealth within.

I have twice visited the north coast of the Dominican Republic. Here the towns and villages are decrepit, despite much downmarket package tourism. The beaches are rocky and often windy, and few have much appeal. Funny to think that on the south-west side of Hispaniola, in Haiti, are some of the most beautiful beaches in the world and not a tourist within miles.

PUERTO RICO

It seems to be a fact of life that the Spanish managed to screw up their colonies. In Puerto Rico they have been aided and abetted by the Americans to produce a mish-mash of Spanish and American culture, if you can call it that - Cortes meets McDonald's. The result is a tropical island version of Florida. The island is big and as you get further from the dreadful San Juan, things do start to get better. But in the end, there isn't much point in going there at all when you would be better off flying to the Virgin Islands just a few miles to the east.

US VIRGIN ISLANDS

St Thomas

This is an attractive island, but very Americanised and, what is worse, inundated with large cruise liners every day of the week. This means the locals are among the most unpleasant people I have ever had to deal with on my travels. The exception is the Indians in the many duty free shops who are helpful, if only in the interests of a sale. (Duty free prices here are possibly the lowest anywhere in the world.) But try getting the time of day from one of the fat mommas in the market near the docks. New York cab drivers are charm personified, by comparison. All of which is a great pity, as Charlotte

Amalia, the capital, is one of the Caribbean's more picturesque towns and the island itself, though somewhat over-developed, makes for a pleasant drive.

St Croix

A former Danish colony that is now an American colony, this place has never fully recovered from the gun massacre of a number of rich whites by disaffected blacks at the golf club in the Seventies. There isn't much in the way of beaches here and, if the island has any charm at all, it is in the colourful Danish buildings that line the seafront of Christiansted, the main town. The locals, though, are only one cut above the people of St Thomas in the friendliness stakes.

St Johns

Definitely the nicest of the three islands in the US Virgin Islands, St Johns is largely owned by members of the Rockefeller clan. The diving around their Caneel Bay resort leaves much to be desired - it's much better on the other side of the island where the coast is extremely hot and barren, but the atmosphere throughout this small, largely undeveloped island is relaxed. The place tends to be expensive, though.

BRITISH VIRGIN ISLANDS

Tortola

The main island in the British Virgin Islands, Tortola might as well be American. The currency is the dollar and most visitors are American. And St Johns is only a couple of miles away in a boat. There isn't much to say about Tortola, except that here the local people compete with the inhabitants of Charlotte Amalia for title of rudest people in the Caribbean. If you ever have the misfortune to be stuck at the island's Beef Island Airport for 24 hours, as I was, you'll understand what I mean. If you are unfortunate enough to ever visit Tortola, get out fast. Fortunately there are other islands in the BVI that are worth visiting.

Peter Island

Peter Island is for the rich only. Like Mustique, it's one of those islands where the visitors are all white, the staff all black. They are shipped in and out each day by boat, leaving the island to its white inhabitants at night. Whatever your view on this kind of set-up, the fact is that Peter Island and nearby Norman Island are a good place to drop anchor if you're on a yacht, as many visitors are. These islands don't have much of an interior, but the diving is okay and the beaches can be a treat.

Virgin Gorda

Very overrated is how I would describe Virgin Gorda and nearby Necker Island. Neither has much in the way of beaches, except for the Baths at the southern end of Gorda, famous for its boulders and sandy coves. It's a favourite spot for a picnic if you've got a yacht and kids. The snorkelling, while it won't set the world on fire, is fun in such clear and friendly water. If only there weren't so many people and boats. Forget about the harbour of North Sound and the nearby hotels, though. It's a good anchorage, but not much else unless you like the American resort approach to vacationing.

Anegada

This is another place I shouldn't even be telling you about. If you want a get-away tropical island in the

Caribbean with some of the best shore snorkelling to be had, this place is paradise in winter. The places to stay (two of them) on the south side are so-so, but the north side of the island, less than an hour away by bike, has wonderful diving off the main reef only 100 yards off-shore. As always, the really serious diving starts once you get over the reef and on to the drop-off. Here you won't be disappointed if you know what you are doing and are prepared to brave the waves. Forget about the small native township further east on the island though - the people will be all but invisible as you pedal through town and will look at you strangely if you ask where you can buy bread.

If you have a boat, head for Horseshoe Reef at the east end of Anegada. This reef stretches a couple of miles off to the south and gets progressively deeper and more exciting. Dive on the drop-off side - again we're talking snorkelling if, like me, you're happy in water up to about 60 feet deep.

Don't expect crowds here. Though Virgin Gorda is only ten miles away across the water, most charter companies won't allow their boats to approach Anegada, the only coralline island in the Virgin Islands, as there are so many reefs and potential bottom hazards. If you do get permission and can stay off the shallow bottom and jagged coral, the experience is one to remember. If you don't like diving, however, forget it.

Jost van Dyke

This island, a couple of hours' sail north of Tortola, is popular with sailors, but don't try and anchor in the one good bay for the night in the high season if you want to be all alone. You're more likely to find yourself bumping into the next boat as you swing on your anchor cable in the middle of the night. Ashore, though, is a good bar and restaurant.

St Martin/Sint Maarten

A small island half-French and half-Dutch is a bit of an oddity to start with. However, it really is true that the two halves are quite different from each other. Perhaps not surprisingly, any charm that there is is all on the French side. This could be due in part to the fact that the Dutch side seems to specialise in cruise traffic and casinos. Either way, it's best avoided.

The French side has the better restaurants and beaches, including a nude beach, though if you really want good beaches, head for Anguilla or nearby Saint Barths.

Saint Barths

This is where the French Rothschilds set up camp years ago. Arguably it's the most expensive and sophisticated island in the Caribbean. Unusually, the white population outnumbers the black. The island is French-speaking and everything costs an arm and a leg, which has successfully kept the package holiday market away. The best way to travel around on this very small island is by rented motorcycle. The whole atmosphere is exclusive - literally. If you don't know anyone, you will end up feeling a bit shut out. However, the best beaches are public and they aren't even crowded. St Barth's is a good place to visit for a couple of days, but unless you have friends like the Rothschilds to stay with, you would find yourself growing bored if you stayed any longer.

Anguilla

Anguilla has deliberately gone for the upper end of the package market in recent years, with hotels to match. The people are fairly friendly and the beaches really are good, compared with say Antigua, which shouts about its 365 beaches, very few of which are worth writing home about. If you want a really out-of-the-way experience, you could head for the eastern tip of Anguilla and get a local fishing boat to ferry you to Scrub Island, where there is a bungalow hotel of sorts in Deadman's Bay. And off Scrub Island is Little Scrub island, uninhabited at the last count, but good if you like to feel you've ended up for the day on an uninhabited tropical island. It really is covered in scrub, though, so you would not want to spend the night. Maybe just an hour's snorkelling would be enough.

ST KITTS

Basseterre, the capital of St Kitts, is a small charming town, so it's a great pity that this once interesting island took the decision a few years ago to get involved in legal gambling. The result, as with Sint Maarten, is that the black *mafia* have got a foothold on the place, and from there it's all downhill unless you happen to be a gambler. There are virtually no good beaches on St Kitts, the most interesting place to go being the well-preserved British naval fortress dating back to the eighteenth century.

NEVIS

Though twinned with St Kitts next door through much of its history, these islands are very different from each other. Nevis is even more lacking in good beaches than St Kitts and the few that there are tend to have black sand and be unpleasantly windy. However, people don't go to Nevis for beach holidays. They go for plantation living, since there are a number of former plantation houses catering to a very upmarket American clientele at prices to match. The emphasis is on genteel tropical living and good food. In fact, many of the plantation houses are not even close to the sea and visitors may need transport to get to the admittedly not very interesting seashore. Nevis, like St Kitts, is steeped in British naval history and it's possible to visit the small church in which Horatio Nelson got married. Of all the places where I have met interesting American visitors in the Caribbean, Nevis comes out top, which must be saying something.

STATIA

Properly known as Saint Eustatius, this island has almost nothing going for it, except for a single small hotel run by two American gays when I was there and serving some of the best food in the Caribbean. The landscape and beaches, though, can readily be given a miss.

SABA

A strange inbred island where they speak Dutch, Saba has one of the world's most extraordinary and dangerous aircraft landing strips. It's built into the side of a hill and landing is like touching down on an aircraft carrier, but without the rubber bands to slow you down. Needless to say, STOL aircraft are preferred here. Don't expect to stay on a place like Saba for more than a couple of days. The place is tiny and surrounded with cliffs, though I've heard a rumour that there's one place where it's possible to swim in the sea.

ANTIGUA

This is one of the most over-hyped islands in the Caribbean. True, English Harbour and Nelson's

Dockyard in the south are worth a day's visit, or a stay of a day or two if you have a yacht. But forget about most of the much-vaunted 365 beaches. Most of them are no big deal. The hotels tend to be nondescript. Ditto the service. For a get-away experience, it's more interesting to head for Barbuda, just to the north.

Barbuda

Barbuda is part of Antigua politically, but there the resemblance ends. Where Antigua is hilly, Barbuda is flat and coralline. It has only one settlement (Codrington), where cheap accommodation can be found. At one end of the island is beautiful Palmetto Point and, nearby, a beach said by some to be the best in the world. While this is arguable, it's true that the clean sandy bottom and clear water take the breath away. However, the best part of the beach (the far end) is monopolised by a very expensive hotel, where they don't take kindly to non-guests going for a swim. I don't believe they have any legal right to control the beach below mean high-water mark, so if you go there bear this in mind. (It's something worth remembering around a lot of coastline where stuck-up hotels pretend to have an exclusive right to bits of beach and water.) If you're the adventurous kind of snorkeller and like wild waters with big fish, the diving on the ocean side of Barbuda is first rate.

GUADELOUPE

Trust the French to have the good life sorted out. Because (like Martinique) Guadeloupe is a French *département*, the inhabitants have all the rights of those living in metropolitan France. This means supermarkets bulging with the best of French food, all imported, of course, and there are endless restaurants and hotels. The roads are good and everything works, which, for the Caribbean, is saying something. However, all this makes for a boring place. There's a volcano and a nude Club Med to spice things up, but all in all Guadeloupe gets the thumbs down for lacking colour and excitement.

DOMINICA

The contrast between this impoverished island and next-door Guadeloupe is what really struck me. From the northern end of Dominica you can look out at its rich French neighbour a few miles to the north. Dominica is still relatively primitive and, when I was there, it had been devastated by a hurricane a few months before. There was almost no tourist infrastructure and, outside the small capital township of Roseau, the only accommodation was of the home-stay variety. This turned out to be a pleasant experience, helped by the fact that my two children were very small at the time, and in most developing countries children can serve as a great ice-breaker with the locals. Dominica was no exception, and the big momma who was our hostess took us down to the beach where we watched as she received her share of a huge leatherback turtle that had been caught and was being shared out between all the inhabitants in the village.

The one drawback in Dominica is that it takes a long time to get anywhere. The roads are poor and they wind interminably among vast acres of banana plantation. Bananas are the main export, and tourism hardly rates, possibly because there are few beaches, and those that there are tend to have black sand.

MARTINIQUE

While Martinique, like Guadeloupe, is a French *département*, it is much less developed than

Guadeloupe. Its port in Fort de France is popular with yachtsmen. I had the experience of being in the town the day after the police had shot two striking plantation workers. The whole island was demonstrating in the streets, and I found myself barricaded in a central bar as hundreds of machete-wielding plantation workers rampaged through the street outside. Fortunately, they were more eager to burn down the police station than cut the throats of a few hapless white tourists. Being a French island, the food can be good on Martinique, and the local girls have the longest legs and shortest skirts I have seen anywhere, apart from Riga in Latvia.

St Lucia

This is another one of those islands full of visitors who have swallowed the tourist propaganda. There are almost no good beaches, the locals can be surly, and a couple of spectacular mountain peaks are, at the end of the day, all that this island has to shout about. I've passed through a couple of times. The first time, I stayed one night. The next time I left the same day.

St Vincent

I would rather spend time here than on St Lucia. The people are definitely not that friendly, but the free diving around the north-east side (the windward side) among the ocean swell is fantastic if, like me, you like to see schools of large fish close inshore. St Vincent also has a volcano in the middle with a lake in it, if you fancy that kind of day excursion.

One of my lasting memories is that in the primitive north of the island there were bare-breasted women, the descendants of slaves like most black people in the Caribbean. These women had not yet got round to covering their breasts in the way of so-called development, yet we had just arrived from Martinique, 70 miles away, where French women were wandering topless on the beaches. Such is the irony of modern travel.

THE GRENADINES

This group of islands and small islets is shared by St Vincent and Grenada. My favourite is Bequia, only a short distance south of St Vincent. The locals are not very friendly - yet again something to do, perhaps, with the large number of cruise ships dropping by - but the island itself, what there is of it, is pretty, not least the harbour where the cruise boats drop anchor. No matter that a couple of tourists had been knifed to death there, the week before I arrived.

A drive across the island brings you through coconut groves to one of the most alive coral reefs I have swum over - alive with fire coral, which burns to the touch, leaving a nasty rash. Beyond it, though, in deeper water, is wonderful snorkelling.

Mustique

Mustique is not far south of Bequia, close enough for the white inhabitants of Mustique to draw on the black population of Bequia for staff. You can see why Colin Tennant picked on Mustique as his upper crust bolthole. It has several very good beaches, the nicest of which, Macaroni Bay, is somewhat spoilt by the wreck of a liner than ran aground on the reef years ago. This is where large numbers of reef sharks allegedly come close inshore during the mating season.

The Cotton House on Mustique is now an expensive hotel and the island is probably a little too well known to be called a hideaway any more. It's a good place to drop anchor for the night for dinner ashore or a drink at the bar on the long jetty.

Tobago Cays

These are truly islets, uninhabited but visited daily by several dozen yachts for no better reason than that they are a pretty day anchorage adjacent to some very good snorkelling.

Palm Island

You could walk round this resort island in a few minutes and I did. It was full of Canadians on package holidays. Their bungalows seemed to circle the entire island. The only object of interest ashore was a large water catchment built of concrete. I could not imagine a more boring place to spend a week or two. If I wanted that sort of thing, I would get it in the Maldives where there is at least some local colour and the diving is better by far.

Union Island

This island really belongs to the locals, who are quite friendly and have managed to stay away from tourism, probably because there is not much in the way of beaches. The main attraction is a shark pool by the dock, and the yacht club does a reasonable Christmas dinner, as I found out.

Carriacou

Once a pirate haunt, Carriacou is a part of Grenada politically. It's quite a big island and has a small township (Hillsborough) where tourists are not made to feel welcome. This may have something to do with the fact that the only tourists they tend to see are relatively rich, since they almost all arrive on yachts. Also the island provides the staff for nearby Petit St. Vincent, a private resort island that is one of the most expensive places to stay in the Caribbean.

Having said that, there is one place worth a few days' stay on Carriacou. I won't tell you its name, but a clue is that it's on the south-east side. It has no beach, but it's only half a mile from White Island, an uninhabited islet that has a glorious white beach on one side and is the hopping-off point for brilliant snorkelling on the other. The hotel has a plantation feel and serves wonderful food in grand style. Rooms are bungalows.

GRENADA

It is difficult to characterise Grenada. All Caribbean islands are different. Perhaps the best way to sum up this one is to say it's like Barbados must have been 40 years ago, but without the rich villas and visitors that Barbados had then.

It takes time to get around Grenada in a hire car, and in that respect it seems a lot bigger than Barbados. Are the people friendly? I would say the answer is a qualified 'yes'. It isn't an expensive island.

The main town (St George's) isn't much to write home about. The beaches vary from good to poor, with most on the poor side (Barbados scores better here).

But all in all, I liked Grenada. It has a quirkiness that would take me back again.

BARBADOS

Over the years, I've been back to Barbados several times and have seen the changes. When I first went there in 1972, it was still the haunt of the rich, whose villas lined the coast of St James's, then as now. Sandy Lane was the place to stay if you were anybody - perhaps more so then, as it was still an independent hotel, not part of an international hotel group as it is now. (My wife learnt to scuba dive in the hotel pool.) Barbados had much to offer then, and a local populace who were and still are on the friendly side, though now they are a good deal better off than they were in the old days.

Barbados to me is the Crane, a favourite spot for body-surfing on the east coast. It's also the old plantation house of Sam Lord's Castle, though that too has been taken over by a big hotel group. It's also surfing at Bathsheba, though I wouldn't want to face the huge crowds of surfers, local and foreign, who go there now. It's the plantation in St John's where I spent hours snorkelling in the wild waters far offshore among the waves. It's the remote northern end of the island near the lighthouse, where the locals were poor and unfriendly. And it's Maycocks Beach north of Speightstown, where Ingrid Bergman is said to have swum unobserved in the Fifties.

There are good beaches all over Barbados (far better than most of those to be found in, say, Antigua), which probably explains its continuing popularity. A pity, though, that Barbados has been discovered by the mass package holiday market in the last 20 years. You can still get away from it all, if you are prepared to brave the rugged east coast. The beaches north of the Crane are not as pretty as on the west coast, but for serious snorkelling far out on the drop-off, the underwater scenery and fish are memorable.

It's a sad fact that tourist rip-offs and petty crime are now endemic in Barbados. Luggage theft seems to be one of the favourites, especially at the airport.

TOBAGO

It used to be that you had to go through Trinidad to get to Tobago. Now you can fly in direct, which is another way of saying that the mass market has arrived. This is a pity, as this is an island that isn't really big enough to handle large numbers without being spoilt. There are good beaches and good snorkelling around the southern and north-east ends of Tobago, but to my mind it's a one-time-only island.

MONTSERRAT

It's a great pity that Montserrat has been devastated by a volcano. Most of its people have been uprooted and the island is now largely uninhabitable. Not that Montserrat had much in the way of visitor facilities. All the beaches except for one are of black sand. The interior scenery that I recall was sparse. But the thing I remember most about the island is how friendly the people were. Having said how unfriendly the locals are to visitors on many Caribbean islands, it comes as a relief to be able to say that this is not always the case. It may have had to do with the fact that I was staying in VSO accommodation and these people were well integrated in the local community. Anyway, I was taken happily by locals on a trip by open boat to visit Rendezvous Bay, the only white sand beach. The skipper sang calypso hits of the Mighty Sparrow the whole way while I chatted up a former Miss Montserrat, along for the ride.

CHAPTER SEVEN
EUROPE

ITALY

My introduction to Italy was Naples in the middle of the night in winter in the mid-Sixties - rats, slums and thieves - but for all that there was a nineteenth-century feel about the place that I liked. In fact, I liked it much more than a visit a quarter of a century later, when all I found was traffic chaos as I tried to locate the motorway south to the Amalfi coast. When I found it, I wished I hadn't. It could not have changed much since Mussolini's time - a narrow bump and grind filled with fuming lorries and an outside temperature in the nineties.

The coast around Amalfi is blessed with mainly small hotels and most of the tourists seem to be local, which is a plus point. But the sea for all its clarity is noticeably lacking in almost anything that lives, a sign of the times in the Mediterranean thanks to decades of pollution and over-fishing.

Rome was in the throes of preparing for Year 2000 when I was there in autumn 1998 and half the historic monuments were off-limits for cleaning and repairs. I hadn't been to Rome before and had expected a more romantic city. The whole place is a pedestrian's worst nightmare. It's not just the legendary speeding drivers who regard every person on foot as fair game. It's the lack of safe crossing points, the pavements that are impassable thanks to building works and the vehicles all over them - that's if there are any pavements at all. Often there are none. Rome is, it seems, a city that has been blighted by traffic like no other, with the possible exception of Budapest.

What's on the plus side for Rome? The Vatican and its museum take first place, followed by walking and sitting at sidewalk cafes in the old district of Trastevere which has come into its own in recent years thanks to a relative shortage of cars to disturb the peace. The

Coliseum is worth a visit about an hour before closing in the autumn, preferably as part of a guided group. At that time the crowds will have gone and it will be relatively cool. However, the Forum and surrounding area are a bit of a disappointment, as is much of the rest of the city. The area around the Trevi Fountain is worst, being a permanent throng of tourists all day long. The Spanish Steps, for two centuries the gathering place for foreigners in Rome, is a little better, and at least you can be sure of buying foreign newspapers there. My final verdict on Rome, as on many cities, is what a pity about the traffic.

By all means drive along the old Appian way to the west of Rome. The ruins of ancient tombs and monuments are there to see, as are a number of prostitutes, mostly black, in short skirts and rouge, plying their trade by the roadside. The Appian Way ends at a motorway, Rome's answer to London's M25. If you dare to find your way through the traffic to the coast at Ostia, don't expect a fishing village. This has got to be one of the ugliest coastal holiday towns in the world, with mile after mile of cheap high-rise apartment blocks that cater to local holiday-makers in the summer. Don't even think about it.

Umbria

The centre of Perugia, the square and surrounding area high in the old town overlooking the countryside, is great - just don't look down on the side where suburban blight spoils the view. There's not much in the way of good places to eat in Perugia and, in fact, not a lot to do except walk around or visit the church. Frankly, there's a better place to visit in Umbria - in the shape of nearby Trevi, which has much in common with the hill towns of Tuscany, with pleasant walks, an old church, and a cafe with outside garden and stunning views over the plain below. They are saying that Umbria will be the place that Brits will move into in droves now that Tuscany is getting too well known. I disagree. The answer, where Tuscany is concerned, is to avoid the better known places in high season.

Assisi

The whole town revolves round St Francis who lived and died here. Assisi has to be one of the prettiest hill towns in Italy, with plenty of hotels to cater for those who turn up without a booking, provided you don't arrive before October. The weather at that time is usually pleasant, as is the atmosphere around the ancient town.

The famous Basilica, which has been restored after earthquake damage, is one of the most fascinating churches I have seen, especially the huge crypt of the saint's tomb. A two mile walk will take you to the Eremo delle Carceri, St Francis's hermitage in the hills above the town. Though the walk is enjoyable through the woods, the hermitage itself is a bit of a disappointment. However you can actually visit St Francis's small stone cell. Assisi has a better range of tourist restaurants than virtually any other hill town I have been to. Most are friendly.

Tuscany

This province deserves its reputation as the nicest part of Italy, if you like beautiful historic places in a rural setting. However, the best time to visit is definitely around October as even September can be busy, especially in Florence and Siena.

My favourite hill town in Tuscany is Montalcino. It's compact and there are a few small hotels that are friendly, if a bit on the expensive side. The harvest season is the best time to be there. Wineries selling the fabled

Brunello di Montalcino are everywhere, as this is the heart of Sangiovese country, and several of the nearby vineyards welcome visitors with tastings, wine museums and visits to their historic houses. However, possibly the best thing about Montalcino is the abbey of Sant' Antimo three miles away, a twelfth-century place, half-ruined and set in green meadows in a valley. Here monks still chant and can be listened to quietly, if you take a seat inside.

Montepulciano, not far away, is a bigger hill town, but equally fascinating, with its old square at the end of a long uphill walk through ancient and once fortified streets. Here too there are small but good (if overpriced) places to stay and enjoy the food and the atmosphere.

I suppose I found Siena disappointing just because it was very crowded, even though this was after the Palio season. The church would have been more interesting had it not been for the fact that they insist on letting in visitors during a service, but shepherding them away from the faithful. Tourists wishing to pray or join the service are let through a rope barrier while hundreds mill noisily around the perimeter. To my mind this just makes for confusion - either you have tourists or you have a service, but not both at once. The local *panforte* is delicious but a good deal cheaper in London than in Siena, where they sell it as though it were caviar rather than a slice of nuts, honey and so forth.

Florence

Florence is best avoided in the busy season, so don't go before October - or before mid-winter if you want to get into the Uffizi without queuing for hours. I haven't yet got inside after three visits to Florence. The Duomo is impressive and fortunately doesn't require much queuing up. However, it does suffer from that growing ecclesiastical disease - turning churches into

133

museums and charging to get in, then charging a bit more to see special bits. Venice is the worst place for this, but it's a worldwide phenomenon that portends the day when all churches will just be museums.

Florence has much to offer despite the petty crime, the inevitable traffic chaos and the narrow streets. Head across the Ponte Vecchio at night to find good cheap eateries frequented by students on the south side of town. The market, though clean and organised, still has character and is worth a visit. Any visitor to Florence should expect prices to be high, especially the hotels. Even cheap places with poky little rooms can leave you feeling poor on departure.

San Gimignano and the Tuscan hill towns

It has become fashionable for Brits to visit or even stay in San Gimignano, a strange-looking hill town notable mainly for its medieval tower houses that go back to a time when important families in the same town used to engage in perpetual feuds and, in consequence, had to fortify their houses. San Gimignano has it all, as well as some of the most expensive hotels you can possibly imagine for rooms that size. However, the best bet if you stay the night is to spot a card in a shop window advertising rooms to let. These are a fraction of hotel prices and often just as nice, especially if, like us, you wake up to autumn mists spread over the valley below.

The streets are filled with shops aimed at tourists. There are probably a couple of dozen places to eat in this small town, and in September they all seem to be full, with prices to match. (It's the time of year for *porcini* mushrooms which feature on all menus around this time.) However, the church is glorious, thanks to its wall paintings - well restored medieval depictions of heaven and hell - and the courtyard behind, where musicians play, can be a real refuge from the streets outside.

The Tuscan countryside

The best thing about Tuscany may in the end be the countryside itself. I had expected it to be more built up when I went there. The fact is that a lot of it, especially Chianti, is very rural and quite wooded, giving the impression of isolation. There are hamlets in Chianti that look unchanged from centuries ago, and small wineries well worth a visit. The town of Greve is not on the foreign tourist circuit, but has an ancient triangular-shaped square, if you can call it that, that evokes a past way of life by the arcaded shops around its three sides. Not that the rest of the town is much to write home about, but it is only a short distance from here to Monte Fioralle, a devastatingly pretty hilltop village with winding streets and an old church.

In contrast, the coastal part of Tuscany is disappointing. Here the countryside isn't a patch on the famous hill towns, with the possible exception of Volterra on the way to the coast, and the beaches themselves are best left to the locals who flock there in the summer.

Venice

There's no denying that Venice deserves at least one visit in a lifetime. The problem is when to go, and my advice is to go in the last week in March, as the tourist season really takes off in the first week of April and continues right through to winter. Prices are not quite full blast at the end of March and, if you are as lucky there as I was, you will encounter spring weather with day-time highs around the 70 degree mark.

While a gondola trip is worth doing once, if you can afford the mortgage, Venice is best seen on foot, followed by ferry trips across the lagoon to places like the Lido (actually best avoided as it's just a beach and there's nothing much to see) or Murano - where the glass museum and a walk around the streets is a pleasant way to spend a few hours after the throng of Venice.

A tour of the Doge's palace and the Basilica in the Piazza San Marco is worth the effort, as is a visit to some of the old churches in Venice to see their paintings. Most restaurants for tourists are around the Rialto Bridge, though as you would expect in a tourist trap, both food and service are poor. To eat well in Venice you really need to go where the locals go, and do some guidebook research beforehand. I was lucky to be offered a complimentary suite on the top floor of the Hotel Danieli and my daughter and I therefore had a good central base from which to spread out for walks and regroup later.

Venice is stunning for one thing above all - apart from the welcome absence of cars. It's the realisation that the place has hardly changed on the outside in several hundred years. Everywhere are images of the city in past centuries and it looked just as it does now. That alone is enough to make Venice special, despite the realisation that this is a town which seems to exist solely to entertain and exploit tourists.

I refused to bribe the porter at the Danieli for a performance of Mozart's *Idomeneo* at Venice's legendary La Fenice opera house, so I didn't get to see it. The place was burnt down a few months later. Poetic justice maybe, though actually it's a great shame that Venice lost an opera house that had remained almost exactly as it was built in the eighteenth century.

SPAIN

There are two Spains as far as I am concerned. One is the tourist Spain of the 'Costas' down the Mediterranean coast. The other is the rest of the country. The first is as dreadful as the latter is charming. I can't claim to know much about the Costa Brava, the Costa del Sol and so on. I drove down the Mediterranean coast road once in August - bumper to bumper at two miles an hour most of the way. All I saw of Barcelona was mile after mile of ugly concrete apartment blocks and I didn't stop, though I'm sure the old town around the port must be delightful. When we stopped for the night, father and two tired kids, at the only hotel that wasn't full, it turned out to be a package holiday place where the staff were thrown into consternation at the sight of independent travellers seeking a bed for one night. Finally they found someone who knew what to do. The next morning I discovered that the bonnet badge had been souvenired from my car.

Further south we ventured on to the legendary Autopista de la Muerte where hundreds die annually, so they say, trying to cross a road where there are no crossing points. We tried to cross it on foot and barely lived to tell the tale. Finally we got to Algeciras and fled by ferry to tranquil Morocco.

However, the real Spain, as everyone knows, is not to be found on the Mediterranean shore any more. My favourite bit of Spain, and the only part I know reasonably well, is the coastal stretch from Irun on the border with France to Cape Finisterre in the west and on down to the River Minho, which forms the boundary with Portugal.

There is good and bad along Spain's northern coast. The bad is Bilbao, despite its new Guggenheim Museum. It is still a dirty old industrial town. And Gijon and Oviedo to the west are not much better. However, San Sebastian, where the Spanish royal court used to spend the summer in the nineteenth century, retains much of its old charm as a seaport. Santander in Asturias, west of the Spanish Basque country, has a beautiful seafront where the old and even some of the young still do the evening promenade along the elegant seafront, giving the impression that not much has changed in 100 years. Only the traffic, growing year by year, spoils the old world effect.

There are many fishing villages along the north coast of Spain and some of the most picturesque are in the Basque country. My favourite is Mundaka, a haunt of surfers in the winter since it has Spain's only surfing spot that is world famous. To get there means going through Guernica, a nondescript town famous for being bombed by Franco in the Civil War, then painted by Picasso, who depicted the suffering of the inhabitants who stood up to the Spanish dictator.

All along the long north coast of Spain there are small fishing villages where the seafood is fresh and cheap and the locals will look at you curiously if you venture into their seafront bars. There are few foreign visitors to this part of Spain and while local Spanish tourism has grown, it is mainly restricted to the summer months.

When I first made the trip westward from Biarritz in 1966, it took three days of bump and grind over roads left over from the dark ages. I only saw one other foreigner the entire way, and got arrested for walking along the road wearing shorts. Times have changed and there is now a nude beach near the spot where I was stopped.

Now the road is much better and much more crowded. It leads eventually to El Ferrol, a town called El Ferrol del Caudillo when I was last there, in deference to El Caudillo, the Generalissimo, Franco himself, who was born there. I believe that in recent times the 'del Caudillo' has been discreetly dropped from the town's name. The best thing about El Ferrol is the *parador*, one of the best in Spain, a seventeenth-century palace that is a glorious place to rest after a long drive.

From El Ferrol it's only a short drive to the city of La Coruña near Cape Finisterre, where there's an ancient village of whitewashed houses perched on the promontory. Don't even try to drive through the streets of this village. They get narrower and narrower until the only way forward is on foot. South of La Coruña, it's a drive of about three hours to the River Minho that forms the boundary with Portugal. There's a bridge to cross over, but in 1966, when I first went there, I camped on the north side and paddled across the river half a mile to enter Portugal illegally, for some surfing around the lighthouse island of Moledo - then paddled back again on my surfboard.

I don't claim to know much of the interior of Spain, but I can vouch for places like Cadiz, Santiago de Compostella, Madrid (if only for the Prado Museum), Granada, Cordoba and Seville (which was partially blighted when I was there, by black smoke drifting across the city from ugly factory chimneys that should have been banned by an EU directive by now).

The drive west from Seville to Portugal is a lasting memory for me, as the old and uncrowded road meanders through orchards, fields and valleys that have something of the Middle Ages about them, evoked by the ruins of medieval castles that pop up near the road.

I went in autumn and it was 20 years ago, so I expect that things will have changed and, as everywhere else, the environment will have been spoilt by too many cars - though I've heard that there is now a motorway from the Algarve to Seville that takes most of the traffic.

Balearic Islands

I spent a lifetime not going to the Balearic Islands, believing they represented all that was worst about mass-market tourism. Then the chance came to spend a week with the kids in Mallorca and another week sailing round Formentera and Ibiza. The attraction was Formentera, described in one guidebook as the last unspoilt island in the Med. So was I pleased or disappointed?

Well Mallorca sure must have been a great place to go when Chopin and Georges Sand were there in 1838, shacking up (to the horror of the locals) at the former Carthusian monastery in Valdemossa. The village is still very pretty today, if a bit inundated with visitors, and the rubbish bins don't get emptied at weekends, so there's litter on the streets.

Mallorca is a very attractive island now ruined by overdevelopment. The fact that it has several miles of three-lane motorway and 7,000,000 visitors a year gives you some idea. Although there are patches of roadway lined with rubbish, most of the island is quite clean - until you get into the water. The *cala*, to use the Mallorquin or Catalan word, is a small cove within a rocky coastline. Viewed from above, most of the *calas* in Mallorca are very tempting turquoise affairs - until you get into them with a mask and snorkel. Out to sea they are fine, but inshore in almost every cove there is a quantity of man-made detritus swilling around, most of it plastic bags of one sort or another.

We stayed in Puerto Andraitx, which I had thought would be relatively unspoilt. Well it must have been nice 30 years ago, but 'unspoilt' is a relative word, and a harbour with a big marina and hundreds of pleasure boats, not to mention dubious water, is not my idea of a getaway kind of place. The accommodation all seems to be aimed at the German middle market and, after all, the Germans are the big investors in Mallorca these days - much of it hot money. There are dockside restaurants at prices that rival anything in London's middle range and haven't a tenth of the atmosphere or bonhomie of the real thing on the islands of Greece and Turkey.

There are a couple of places relatively free of pollution that are worth a visit for a swim. One is the Cala Figuera in the north, two or three miles beyond the beach at Formentor. It's popular with boats and a bit stark (no beach - just rocks), but as a swimming and snorkelling spot it's one of the best on the island. Perhaps even better in the south-east of the island is the Cala de s'Almonia. It's how the *calas* of Mallorca all were once, and maybe the only reason it has stayed clean, picturesque and uncrowded is that the locals have made a big effort to remove all the road signs pointing the way there. I'm not going to spoil it for them now by telling you how to find it, but if you do manage ever to go there, you may feel, as I did, that it's the best thing Mallorca still has to offer.

But on to Formentera, via a 12-hour passage in a charter sailing boat. That at least was fun. We arrived at our real goal, the last unspoilt island, to find the remote southern beach of Migjorn covered in hotels and package holiday-makers. I had forgotten the prime caveat where guidebooks are concerned - since they all copy each other, no one is ever up to date and the description you'll be reading may be telling you what the place was like eons ago. In the case of Formentera, this was certainly true. So we made the easy decision not to go ashore, as the sea looked a lot more tempting anyway. Instead we did the sensible thing and concentrated on small uninhabited offshore islets, of which there are a few round Formentera and more off Ibiza. Around Formentera these didn't prove to be all that exciting and I won't bore you with them, but we did move on to Ibiza, just to the north - that island most famous for the world's largest disco and lager louts by the square yard.

W e didn't go ashore here either, though with an extra day, we might well have visited the old town of Eivissa and its well-preserved historic architecture. The inebriated masses are, after all, to be found on the other side of the island around Sant Antoni. In fact, it was on an island only ten miles out from Sant Antoni that we found the best snorkelling in the whole region (we tried a lot of uninhabited islets, so we're in a fair position to judge). I'm not going to put a name to it and I've given too many clues already. We thought we had the place to ourselves when we anchored, but two or three small boats came and joined us. If you're used to snorkelling in coral waters, the Med will always be a disappointment, but here the visibility was a good 70 feet and I saw what I have never seen in inshore waters in the Med before - real fish, a couple of them about two feet long, to add to the thousands of scissor tails and other small school species. In all, we sailed almost 200 miles by the time we got back to Palma, Mallorca.

I wouldn't go back to the Ballearics, as I can't see the greed that has led to overdevelopment ever being reversed. Palma is a clean and charming town - if only the whole island wasn't swamped with cars and people. It's happening in the same way in the Canaries, and in Madeira it's already beyond a joke. When will they ever learn? Oh and one thing more, if you must go to the Ballearics, go around March or October and avoid the heat as well as the crowds - it's around 90 in the shade for most of August.

PORTUGAL

I'm not wild about Lisbon. It's a bit like a poorer version of Madrid. Oporto has much more charm, as do the northern towns and villages along the coast, starting with Ericeira, an hour's drive north of Lisbon. (I don't have a lot to say for Cascais - too developed - but Guincho further north is where the coastline begins to get primitive and interesting.) The coastal towns that are worth a visit to the north of Ericeira are Peniche, Nazare, Figuera da Foz and Viana do Castelo. They still depend to some extent on fishing, and the seafood in the small local restaurants can be good if you know what to order. This is more easily said than done, as it means fighting your way past the standard menu that is offered by every average Portuguese restaurant - green vegetable soup, cod (or pork or chicken) and crème caramel pudding. If you can get away from this menu, you can eat well. The standard menu, however, is usually boring.

When I first went to Northern Portugal, widows in black leading a cow along the road or riding on a donkey were still a common sight. Now they are all but gone, even in remote parts, and cars are everywhere, especially in the south, for the south is richer (and less conservative) than the north.

The Algarve would be better without so much traffic to spoil its pretty towns and coastline. Between Lisbon and the Algarve, coastal Portugal is very underdeveloped and a bit of a no-man's-land. The western Algarve, however, north of Sagres, is interesting, if you like to find remote cliff-top walks and wild rocky beaches with little sign of human life. Cape Saint Vincent itself, which forms the corner of Portugal (and Europe for that matter) just west of Sagres, has many associations with the Peninsular War and is an interesting place to explore with its old fortress and cliff-top views.

CZECH REPUBLIC

The Czech Republic isn't all Prague, and Prague isn't all the old centre of the city, though there is a tendency for visitors to see things that way, as though England were all Piccadilly Circus and Buckingham Palace. There are two places outside Prague that I have been to, both famous for their castles - Karlstejn and Krivoklat. The former is somewhat over-hyped and the atmosphere spoilt by hustlers and hawkers around the parking area down below. The less touristy Krivoklat is a different matter. Here is a castle that has a real dungeon, in which were found real skeletons when its sealed door was broken down some years ago. The story of the castle and its noble lady who lived above, while her enemy rotted (alive) for years below, is fascinating. If you go anywhere outside Prague in the Czech Republic, this is the place to go - it's about two hours' drive from the city.

Prague is such a beautiful city that it's a pity that the famous Wenceslas Square in the middle is rapidly becoming a Czech version of Leicester Square and equally tawdry. Outside this square, with its hotels that match London and Paris in price if not in quality, the old town has been and is still rapidly being restored. Prague is on a roll and you can feel it everywhere you go. They almost shook off the Russians in 1968 and now that they have finally done so, they are not looking back as they rush into capitalism, good and bad.

I wasn't left with an impression of good food in Prague, though there are plenty of pleasant places to eat. It's the architecture that really grabs visitors, especially the ancient and beautiful Charles Bridge and, on the other side, the enormous edifice of Prague Castle. Most impressive is the huge wooden-floored hall where courtiers once pranced around on horseback. I've always been fascinated by the fact that in the sixteenth and seventeenth centuries Bohemia, and Prague in particular, was Europe's centre of political liberalism and spiritual learning, and attracted innovative Protestant thinkers from the rest of Europe. When you drive out of Prague on the motorway, though, you pass through miles of dreary suburbs that make you realise that the real day-to-day Prague of the local people is like everywhere else - drab, boring and polluted.

HUNGARY

There is one problem in Hungary. Turn up in a BMW or a Mercedes or something of that ilk and you will spend a lot of time worrying that you may never see your wheels again. Car crime is big in Hungary and especially in Budapest. Park your pride and joy in the wrong place at the wrong time and it may well be gone before you can say Russian *mafia*. I stayed at the big and pleasant Ramada Grand Hotel on Margaret Island in the middle of the river in Budapest, thinking my car would be safe there. Well it was, but only because I paid a lot of money to have it put in the guarded underground car park. It seems that cars have a habit of disappearing from in front of the hotel itself, even though they have to pass through mechanical barriers and over a bridge to leave the island - on their way no doubt to Moscow or St Petersburg.

The hotel had big rooms and very friendly and helpful staff, for a place that size. They were willing to make reservations for you at the front desk with no obvious expectation of a tip - far better than any comparable big hotel in Western Europe that I can think of, since the service seemed genuinely friendly. There was even a hot spa in the basement of the adjoining building and mostly local people lounging in the warm waters. Taking the waters is still a big thing in Budapest.

However, there is another vehicle-related negative in this city, and that is the cars that are parked all over the pavement - so many at all hours of the day and night that getting around on foot is a pain in the neck. These are not BMWs inviting the attention of some *mafioso*, but your regular old Trabants - that kind of thing - which a *mafioso* would not take home to Moscow if you paid him to.

Budapest has its Royal Palace high on a hill overlooking the city and, apart from that, not a lot going for it in comparison, say, with Prague. There is one exception, however. Apart from the Gellert Baths (worth a look if not a swim), Budapest has one of the world's most interesting restaurants, the Gundel, located behind the Museum of Fine Arts and best reached by taxi. It has been restored by an émigré Hungarian who made a fortune in America, and it serves the best food in the city at prices which, though high by Hungarian standards, are no more than your average for a reasonably good meal out in London. The small baroque palace that is the restaurant is what makes this place special, together with the live music (especially the standing violinist in his tailcoat) that adds a touch to the place to make it feel as though you have stepped back into Budapest - or Paris for that matter - in the middle of the nineteenth century. The place is just a little bit self-conscious and so are the diners, mostly foreigners, but that is the only negative.

The Hungarian countryside, however, is disappointing, especially compared with the Czech Republic, and even outside Budapest your car may be at serious risk.

SWEDEN

Best time to go is winter if you are staying with Swedes. Snow is everywhere and the Christmas trees are growing right there in the ground. Those in people's gardens are lit at night with real candles since the air is often still.

Roads are dangerous to drive on, though, at this time of year. Like most of Scandinavia, everything is clean and well ordered and just a little bit too clinical to be other than boring, if you're like me and like life to be a bit on the wrong side of predictable.

DENMARK

Much like Sweden and equally expensive. The Walking Street in Copenhagen is something there should be more of in all European cities, It has been around since the Sixties at least and has been imitated with varying success all over the world. London could certainly do with more of the same, starting with somewhere like Piccadilly or Beauchamp Place.

HOLLAND

The feeling you get on visiting Amsterdam is that here is a city where there's no one in charge. Apart from the graffiti everywhere, and the confusion of road lanes that seem to exist for everything from bikes to prams, I like the place. The people are easy-going. It's only when you get out in the country and head for the coast that you begin to realise that while all that flatness may be good for bicycling, it can be deadly boring.

Best thing to see in Amsterdam is the Van Gogh Museum, where the paintings are original and not just copies, despite their astronomical value. Forget about the legal drugs and licensed bordellos, unless that sort of thing really is your cup of tea.

BELGIUM

The Belgian countryside I don't know. The centre of Brussels is still very quaint, which is nice, and even the fact that centuries of grime has not been removed from most of the historic buildings, as it has in other European cities, actually adds to the charm. If you like eating, there is a square in the middle of town where everywhere seems to sell fresh seafood. The high prices are a reflection of all those EU fat-cats living in this city and dining out every day on their big expense accounts. The square with the town hall is impressive for its ancient buildings that look across a cobbled expanse that has changed very little over time.

AUSTRIA

The centre of Vienna is as interesting as the rest of the city is dull and ugly, so it's best to stick to the centre and walk around. As ever, September and October are the best months to visit. The hotels around Vienna are hideously expensive and the food could be a lot more interesting, but the old architecture is a treat, especially the cathedral. Outside Vienna, aside from the ski resorts (St Anton and Lech are the best in the Vorarlberg, otherwise Murren and Wengen), the place to head for is undoubtedly Salzburg, to my mind possibly the most beautiful city in the world, alongside Edinburgh and Paris. Salzburg reeks of Mozart and eighteenth-century baroque. The architecture and the music are everywhere. Fortunately, they have got the traffic under control in the old town - by banning most of it - and it makes all the difference. In fact, there are big lessons to be learnt by other European cities. All the quaintness is a big draw for tourists, with the result that the old part of the city, rather like Venice or Florence, tends to live off it. However, they have done it pretty well if you don't mind the high prices and the fact that hotels get booked up for the season months in advance. The overall feeling I got from Salzburg, especially after visiting the grave of Mozart's wife, is that Mozart was there almost yesterday - not two centuries ago. That's the effect you get when a place hasn't changed much to look at in 200 years and modern intrusions like cars are kept out of the way.

SWITZERLAND

I think people are right when they say Switzerland is boring. It's a good place to ski (I prefer Davos, Verbier and Zermatt), but otherwise it's simply a good place to fly to (Geneva) in order to rent a car and drive off to the French Alps. Towns like Geneva are clean and pretty.

In fact, looking at Swiss towns (if only England were as clean), it's hard to understand why they have such a serious drug problem, unless boredom and the predictable and ordered Swiss lifestyle drives them to it.

GREECE

Central Athens is a noisy polluted place with far too many cars, most of them belching fumes from engines that would fail an emissions test in most of the rest of the EU. Combine this with high summer temperatures and you get a good reason to avoid the place before about October. Athens has little self-evident history on show, apart from the Parthenon, and if I am in Greece in summer I much prefer to be sailing a yacht somewhere out among the islands.

Dodecanese

This island group is just off the Turkish coast. Avoiding Rhodes and Kos, most of the islands are quite pleasant and unspoilt and best visited by hopping from one to another on the local ferry service and finding a place to stay in each port on arrival. The best of the islands are Simi, Kalimnos, Patmos and Samos.

Sporades

This is my favourite group of Greek islands, if you don't count touristy Skiathos, though even this island has its charms if you get away from the hordes.

The islands start to get interesting with Skopelos which, despite a polluted harbour, has possibly the prettiest seafront of them all, with lots of space for the many quayside tavernas that are where everyone eats out in the evening. Beyond Skopelos is the island of Alonissos, where its one tiny port gives the place a pioneer feel, and you get the impression that the whole island is yours, which it is basically. This feeling becomes even more intense if you sail over to nearby uninhabited Peristera, with its many empty bays where you can laze and skinny-dip all day if the fancy take you. Here, too, are caves that you can swim into and snorkel in 30 feet or so of clear, clean water.

The last island going out east in the Sporades is the so-called Cyclops island of Pelagonisi, where you can only just land from a boat on the steep shore. There is only one inhabitant on the island, a local shepherd who will show you the Cyclops cave in return for a nominal tip. It's a bit of a climb, but the cave is interesting and contains the skeleton of a long dead sheep at the bottom of a pit.

The island of Skyros to the south is well away from the others in the group and is where the poet Rupert Brooke is buried. The beaches here are not particularly interesting, but Atsitsa is. This is an English-run New Age centre that offers holidays combined with courses in everything from meditation to yoga, chanting and dance therapy. However, the only satisfying way to visit the Sporades is in a boat, and the best area to take it to is Skopelos and the islands beyond.

Saronic Gulf

This group of islands isn't bad, but doesn't compare with the Sporades. You need a yacht to get around. Undoubtedly the prettiest of the group is Hydra, with its charming but expensive port and dockside cafes that thrive day and night in the warmer months. However, visitors should try to avoid Hydra before October at all costs. A walk round the headland takes you to spots where locals and visitors swim and dive from the rocks, and the water is relatively clean.

The other islands in the group such as Poros and Spetses (the setting for John Fowles's novel *The Magus* - a favourite of mine) are less charming.

TURKEY

My experience of Turkey is limited to sailing the coastline out of Marmoris, and from a sailing point of view this is probably as good as it gets in the Med, as the winds blow strongly here in the summer. The coastline is wild, but filled with good coves and beaches to anchor off, and there are many small restaurants on the shore, often only reachable by boat (many are on off-shore islands). Marmoris itself is a package holiday Mecca, which says it all, but the islands should not be dismissed. They rival the Greek islands in every respect for sailing, with the added advantages that the restaurants are cheaper and the people much friendlier.

CROATIA

I have sailed on this coast and stayed in one of the small fishing villages. Compared with sailing in Greece and Turkey, sailing in Croatia is a disappointment. The people seemed indifferent and sometimes sullen and the sailing territory, while it had its moments, was not brilliant. This was before the troubles that have blighted the whole area in recent years, and I haven't been back since Croatia became an independent state. Maybe things are looking up and the people are starting to smile at last.

LATVIA

Riga must have been a very pretty city in the last years of the nineteenth century, since it has some of the best Art Nouveau architecture in the world. The trouble is that during their long and unwelcome occupation since the Second World War, the Russians have utterly ruined the place, putting up ugly buildings all over the city, with the result that today it's an architectural hodgepodge, with here and there the odd oasis of a stylish building or even a whole block left intact despite the communist devastation. Even at the nearby coast, where the beach looks clean but the smell will put you off swimming, there are a couple of miles of grand villas belonging to another age and in various stages of dilapidation and renovation. Many of these once beautiful structures are now beyond the point of salvation. Riga does have a few old bits left where there are outdoor cafes and a very cheap meal can be had, though you would not want to write home about the standard of the food. The best thing on view is the pretty girls in their short skirts and high heels, their legs of the long variety that goes all the way to the armpits.

In the countryside are the collapsing remains of collective farm buildings, Russian tank ranges, and vast housing blocks. These still accommodate the wives and children of Russian soldiers who have moved home but left their families behind, since there is nowhere to put them up in Russia. The Russians in Latvia (and they are a large minority in the population) are despised and treated like second-class citizens, though many of them have no home other than Latvia and have lived there all their lives.

The city of Riga struggles to be a part of the Western world and, for what it is worth, Latvia aspires to join the EU in a few years. It has an opera house that is said to be cheap and good, and there is a growing number of shops, run by local *mafiosi*, selling goods which the Latvians regard as luxuries but which we in the West would consider as the normal stuff we get from supermarkets.

Riga gets a thumbs-down now (even the Latvian countryside is flat and boring, apart from the lakes among the pine forests) and will probably continue that way, unless one day it is possible to restore the city by tearing down the ugly Russian buildings that are such a blight.

IRELAND

One of Europe's best-kept secrets, southern Ireland has to be one of the most enjoyable countries to visit, provided that it isn't raining, which admittedly is asking a lot. When the sun does shine it is glorious. I'm talking about the counties in the west, such as Donegal, Sligo, Clare and Kerry. I'm not so keen on Dublin. How could they have allowed such a charming city to be spoilt by fast-food outlets all over the city centre, filling the streets with the detritus of hamburger cartons? Head west from Dublin for the Atlantic coast and you'll find the people are friendly, the grass is green and the roads are still not too busy with cars - though the people are getting richer thanks to EU handouts, so the good times, for visitors at least, are unlikely to last.

If you ever knew Cornwall about 40 years ago, that is the kind of feel you get in the coastal areas of Western Ireland - big sea, big sky and country lanes that you can still enjoy driving along. If you go outside the summer season, there is usually a place to stay. If you go armed with the right guide book, farm B & Bs are the answer.

The sea is cold, though, even in summer, which means wetsuits if you're a surfer like me. If you're not, you'll probably just look at the water and go for long walks along the empty shore.

GERMANY

It took me until the late Nineties to visit Germany for the first time, and when I did I was pleasantly surprised, not just to find that the UK really isn't the centre of the universe, but also that there is much about Germany to envy if you live in the UK. On average the (West) German standard of living is superior to Britain's, notwithstanding the upheavals of reunification. I haven't visited former East Germany and maybe I wouldn't say that if I had. But I was impressed with the fact that the roads are always in good condition, there never seem to be any roadworks and motorway holdups, most places are spotlessly clean (none of the litter that blights UK roadsides) and the streets are generally safe to walk at any time of day or night.

I'd been seduced by the film of Mario Lanza in *The Student Prince* years ago, so Heidelberg was a must. It turned out to be a bit of a disappointment but at least the castle had one thing that fascinated me, the biggest wine barrel in the world, called the Grosses Fass. It seems as big as a house and must have held a lot of wine once upon a time (reputedly 221,726 litres). While the university area below the castle has a few interesting squares and cafes and a pleasant lack of traffic, it just doesn't have much life, but I suppose if it had been term time in the winter, with students filling the streets and snow all around, I would have been ecstatic.

The ancient walled town of Rothenburg is fascinating, especially the torture museum (the Medieval Criminal Museum). I hadn't realised that an Iron Maiden was a nasty metal contraption into which miscreants were placed and crushed by its many spikes as it was closed, whereupon this person-shaped frame and occupant, dripping with blood, would be hung on a gibbet as a warning to others. Rothenburg has good, inexpensive and friendly hotels, mainly family-run places. There are not too costly restaurants, and the only Christmas shop in the world - a shop open all year selling nothing but Christmas decorations. There are many visitable buildings and museums, one with the oldest kitchen in the world, part of a nunnery where, in the twelfth century, nuns gave food to the poor through a purpose-built hole in the wall.

Munich has a cathedral that is huge but disappointing. In fact Munich itself, which is highly prosperous, is somewhat lacking in real atmosphere for the visitor, even in the people-filled centre where locals are more in evidence than foreigners. There are plenty of good hotels, a good opera house and theatre, and street stalls selling fresh fruit and vegetables. In the evening, the beer halls with their cheap eateries come alive. The beer is predictably good in these places, the food plentiful but poor. You get what you pay for. However, the road from Munich to Salzburg on a sunny day is a real stunner for its Bavarian mountain scenery.

A trip by road along the Rhine is a disappointment if, like me, you have secretly harboured for years an image of Lorelei and romantic castles. For one thing, you did not imagine there would be a railway line along the river bank and, worse still, overhead power lines for the trains. The river is on the muddy side and looks suspiciously polluted. However, the Rhine does have its redeeming features, especially in autumn when it's harvest time. There are small towns built around the wine industry. Two of the most interesting are the wine towns of St Goar and Rudesheim. There are numerous places to taste and buy, and it's my belief that Riesling, one of the local favourites, is the most underrated and undervalued grape variety in the world as far as top-end dry wines are concerned. There is a wonderful hotel to stay at, called Rheinfels Castle. It is still a castle in many of its parts. You can stay there, eat there with a splendid view of St Goar and the Lorelei Rock, and wander round the ruins and cellars of the castle and its museum.

Further along the river on the other side is the former Cistercian monastery of Eberbach with its stunning twelfth-century architecture. It was here that *The Name of the Rose* was filmed with Sean Connery.

ICELAND

I have only visited Iceland in winter. The capital, Reykjavik, is a bleak grey place at that time of year, though since there are no trees it cannot be all that green in the warmer months.

However, to judge by photos I have seen of Iceland in summer, with its wild waterfalls, rivers and lakes, it might well be worth a camping trip in July or August.

There isn't much to do in Iceland in winter except eat (fish), drink (beer) and watch the many pretty girls around the capital. It is said that Iceland has the pretti-est girls in the world and, having seen for myself, I tend to think this may be no exaggeration.

FRANCE

Paris

What can I say that's new about Paris? I lived there as a student in the late Sixties, and like most of the world's cities I reckon that Paris has only got worse since then. The reasons are many, but traffic and pollu-tion have to be the main explanation why cities are not what they once were, and Paris is no different.

Paris to me is walking the streets of the Left Bank, looking for somewhere full of locals, to find a good meal or a cup of coffee. It's Paris in the proverbial spring, or the autumn, but never in summer, even if the city has been abandoned by the natives and left to the tourists. Paris without Parisians, however rude they get, just isn't Paris.

Paris is also the area around the Sacré Coeur, where I lived near the Porte Saint Denis. It's the little cheese shop on the Ile Saint Louis where I and President Pompidou used to buy the same brand of (unpas-teurised) Camembert, though I have no idea whether it's still there.

Paris is the Louvre - too big by far to visit properly in a single day. It's the modern art Musée d'Orsay that's worth seeing just for the architecture of a converted nineteenth-century railway station. There's always something still to see in Paris. For me it's the Invalides and Napoleon's tomb. And a visit to the opera house which I've only driven past.

But the Puces, the Paris flea market, was not the bar-gain hunter's paradise that I remembered when I recent-ly went there again.

Biarritz, Bordeaux, the Basque country and the Landes

This is where I spent three summers in my student days, surfing and improving my French. In the Sixties it was everything that I could want in a holiday spot. I have been back several times over the years and, sadly, I have seen the place go downhill on each occasion. The problem is traffic, especially in the summer months. But Biarritz has another problem. The whole area to the north - the Landes that stretch all the way to Bordeaux and the Arcachon Basin - has become the scene of massive holiday home development in the last 30 years. The hinterland around Biarritz has gone the same way. The invasion of people - to live and to visit - in what was once an unspoilt part of France, has led to a network of roads and motorways that takes the pleasure out of visiting this spectacular region, with its Basque village hinterland and Basque fishing ports. Biarritz, and by that I mean the whole Basque region around Biarritz, is still worth one visit, but not the longer stay that it once deserved.

However, the ancient town of Bayonne, only five miles from Biarritz, merits a special mention. Its port, at the estuary of the River Adour, is ugly, but the old town a couple of miles up the river has been well preserved and there is plenty of parking space, making a walk round the narrow ancient streets a must if you are in the neighbourhood. It's not unlike Bordeaux on a smaller scale. And Bordeaux itself is worth the trip, just to visit the wine-growing areas around the city. The ancient village of Saint Emilion, above all, is the place to go in this region. Bordeaux, or at least its ancient centre, is interesting, but for my money I'd rather see Bayonne. To really explore the French Basque country, the best base is the small pretty town of St Jean Pied de Port. It's virtually on the border with Spain and if you explore the wine-growing villages in the neighbourhood you may find, as we did, some wonderful undiscovered local wines made by growers whose first language is still Basque.

Annecy

If you drive from Geneva into the French Alps to ski, you will go through this beautiful town on the edge of a stunning lake. I have not stayed here - only passed through - but I've heard good reports, and if you like alpine towns with clean air and a view, it could be worth a stay. It reminds me of Anita Bruckner's novel *Hotel du Lac*.

French Alps

I only know this area from skiing trips in winter, having stayed in Courchevel and Val Thorens. I actually prefer the latter. The architecture is modern and functional and therefore abominable, but the skiing from what is deemed the highest resort in the Alps is outstanding. I've also stayed in La Plagne and skied there and in nearby Avoriaz. Don't expect the pretty scenery of alpine Austria, but the skiing is great for intermediates.

Provence

It's the light in late summer that I always remember most about Provence. That and the fresh fruit in the street markets. It's no wonder that artists flocked there in the last century. I'm not going to list all the places you could go in Provence - there are too many. However, I would stay in Provence rather than crowded and over-priced Cote d'Azur towns any day. Not for me Monte Carlo, Cap d'Antibes, Nice, Cannes and St Tropez, especially not in summer. The Camargue, too, is disappointing, ruined by cars and hordes of mainly French tourists.

I drove through Avignon, Montpellier, Beziers and Nimes and now I wish I had stopped, if only for the Roman ruins.

The Pyrenees

However, if you keep going west through the south of France you eventually come to the Pyrenees. Maybe things have changed since, but I remember once being the only visitor in the small town of Saint Girons, on the French side of the border, and the occasion was memorable - dancing the night away in the cellars of an eleventh-century *château* to celebrate a wedding. I am sure there must still be unspoilt villages deep in the Pyrenees, in Spain as well as in France. Nearer to Biarritz there is Sare and the nearby Basque villages, well worth visiting in autumn, when only the Basque-speaking locals and resident incomers remain.

Alsace

It may be part of France and the language may be French, but the feel of the ancient villages of Alsace is definitely German. 'Picture postcard' is the only way to describe villages like Riquewihr and Roufflach. And the only time to go there is during the vintage in October. The smell of grape must is everywhere, the food excellent and the prices reasonable. Even some of the locals are friendly. Alsace has got to be one of the real gems of Europe and it has yet to be fully discovered by the tourist hordes.

Normandy and Brittany

Angers is a small town in Brittany not far from the Loire and the best concentration of castles in France. I remember it from my stay in the ancient wing of an ancient *château*. The loo was a hole in the wall over the moat far below. So much for French plumbing. I was there in winter and not a soul in sight - at least not another foreign visitor.

However, I have been back to Brittany and Normandy more recently, and I made the mistake of going in August. Never again. Bumper to bumper traffic throughout the country roads of the whole of France, or so it seemed, made this a nightmare experience. Attempts to drive along the Oléron peninsula and to visit Mont Saint Michel were abandoned. The moral: simply do not visit France under any circumstances before the middle of September. The country has been blighted by three things: traffic, outdoor advertising and American fast food. Drive into Nantes from the north and you will see what I mean. You might as well be entering Indianapolis (yes, I have been there), where at least you would find less of a traffic problem and no parking hassles at all.

CHAPTER EIGHT
INDIAN OCEAN

MAURITIUS

Mauritius has become fashionable in recent years as an upmarket package holiday destination. As such, to my mind, it is overrated. There are a few nice beaches. However, Mauritius is more fun as an independent travel destination linked in with other Indian Ocean islands.

I have been to Mauritius three times and each time I have found the south-west end, around Le Morne, more interesting than the more developed areas on the west and north coasts. There is something about Mauritius that tends to remind me of Barbados, though in Mauritius the population is far more mixed, with a broad blend of white, negro, Chinese and Indian. The capital Port Louis is no big deal, though the market is not bad as markets go. The island in size is slightly bigger than Barbados, and the population is more concentrated on the coast, though there is a high interior north of Port Louis that attracts serious walkers.

I can never see the point of going to a single hotel and spending all my time encapsulated there, away from the reality of a country. Yet that is what most visitors seem to do. On the other hand, there are not a lot of places of historical interest.

The game-fishing is said to be good if you like killing sailfish. The diving, however, is only so-so. I would go back to surf - it's good in the south-west - but nothing else would draw me back

RODRIGUES

Officially a part of Mauritius, Rodrigues is a couple of hundred miles or more to the east and a small, relatively undeveloped island. However, when I went there it was not developed at all and the only place to stay was the turn-of-the-century Cable and Wireless building, converted into a small guesthouse with a couple of rooms. In fact, visitors were so scarce that the local representative of Air Mauritius not only met us off the plane but took all four of us home to meet the family and serve us a delicious Chinese meal of grilled fish. How many airlines do that when you land?

We found Rodrigues curious. For one thing, it has its own version of the dodo - the solitaire bird, now also extinct (for the children we made a great play of looking for it, in case there was one left hiding somewhere). There were other European faces on the island - a group of Belgian nuns who ran a small convent and were eager to gather news of the outside world. In fact, they were as delightful as the airline man and his family. Ultimately, it is people that make a place for me more than anything and, as you can tell, the vibes were good on Rodrigues, though the snorkelling, which looked promising, was a bit on the disappointing side.

I believe that now there are at least ten small hotels and guesthouses on Rodrigues, so obviously the place is no longer undiscovered. I would certainly rate it worth two or three days' stay for anyone visiting Mauritius.

REUNION

Because Reunion, like Guadeloupe and Martinique, is a French *département*, it has a high cost of living and an equally high standard of living. For that reason it does not need to rely on tourist revenues like nearby Mauritius. In fact, the two islands are totally different. Reunion has quite a lot in common with Madagascar to the west and there are daily flights between the two.

You would not go to Reunion for its beaches in the normal course of events. It has very few of note, though it does have a famous surf spot - St Leu. The offshore diving on the east coast is good if you like rough water and eerie drop-offs, but is not for the faint-hearted. As for the west coast, it is a mournful-looking shore with little to attract the visitor. Reunion has a reputation for sharks, especially in the south. The biggest tourist draw, if you can call it that, is a long road up a valley to within a mile or so of a live volcano. The cafe at the end of the road (you walk after that) is pleasant and there are never more than a few visitors. The capital itself, St Denis, is a bizarre-looking place with the town cemetery at the northern end of the main street, overlooking the sea, its grounds filled with a whole town full of family mausoleums. You can't miss it. Friendly natives? Yes, reasonably friendly if you speak French, though I'm not sure how it would be if you didn't. Possibly very similar to Madagascar, though the locals in Reunion are much richer, relatively speaking, than their neighbours on the bigger island - and their neighbours in Mauritius too, for that matter.

SEYCHELLES

This pretty group of islands was taking off touristically in the early Seventies when a left-wing revolution put a sudden end to all that and the country became a client state of the USSR. This, of course, turned out to be a disaster economically and set the country's development back many years. When I was there it was still under the communist thumb and in every village children were marching up and down dressed as Young Pioneers. Those locals daring to tell you what they thought hated it all.

Mahe

The main island even then had a lot of tourist hotels and no doubt many more have been built since the Russians left. However, the Seychelles have never quite recovered the dazzling future that looked in store before the Russians took over and made this their Indian Ocean naval base while they looked round for something more permanent. As a result, Mauritius was able to creep in and fill the gap for an upmarket Indian Ocean destination, especially as Sri Lanka, the other contender, ran into problems of its own in the early Eighties. That just left Mauritius and the Maldives to slug it out, with the Maldives winning with the German market and Mauritius with the British. Mahe has the most hotels of the developed islands in the Seychelles, though surprisingly few good beaches, compared with Praslin and La Digue, for example. Victoria, the capital, is small and pretty and is the base for charter boat facilities. However, for a more interesting holiday in the Seychelles, a visitor should do three or four islands, and I would not spend more than a couple of days on Mahe.

Praslin

Home to the erotic coconut that looks like a woman's thighs, this island is fairly undeveloped and has one or two very good beaches, if you don't mind the sea urchins. I got one in my heel that only came out, suddenly, six months later as I was soaking in a hot bath. It was very painful for the first couple of days after it went in. Praslin is the only place I have come across sea urchins in the middle of empty sand - you usually find them on rocks and coral. Bear in mind that, as with many tropical islands, there is not much to do that isn't connected with the sea. Praslin has a very small population, so you may not even come away with an impression of the local people at all.

La Digue

This is undoubtedly the prettiest island of the Seychelles and must be one of the prettiest tropical islands in the world. Transport is by ox-cart from the dock. A short walk takes you over to the other side of the island where swimming is a dream among the inlets set in the giant granite boulders that everyone has seen in photos. There was no one in sight anywhere on that coast when I was there, and my six-year-old son and I spent an hour climbing the rocks.

Maybe these days it is a bit more developed. There isn't much to actually do on La Digue, but that being true of all the Seychelles islands, I would rather enjoy a bit of *farniente* on this island than the others.

Bird Island

You can stay on Bird Island, but I wisely chose the day trip in and out, not being a bird-watcher. In any case, most of the millions of terns that nest here had left by the time we arrived. However, the sea near the hotel and airstrip is a dream of a tropical hot bath, where you can safely walk out 100 yards and still have your head above water. All around is an ocean of clean white sand, though it's not snorkelling territory at this spot as there is literally nothing in the water but the sand underfoot.

MALDIVES

These islands are on my list for a return visit. A lot of development has gone on since I was there 20 years ago, and what seemed adventurous then may not be so now. On the other hand, where you went was much less restricted then. The Maldivian government have tried to protect the islands by defining those which can be visited at all, apart from those designated for tourist hotels. When I was there, you could visit any uninhabited island, and any island inhabited by locals provided you got the headman's permission.

I hired a local boat skippered by a young German and we sailed far to the north of the two atolls around Male, the capital, to which tourism is largely restricted (apart from Gan, the southernmost atoll). The boat took us to Kureddu, then a German diving outpost with six overnight huts on the beach. The diving there and along the way was possibly the best I have come across anywhere. For Napoleon wrasses it was a diver's dream. I wonder if it is still as good after all these years, when so many more visitors will have passed through. Somehow I doubt it.

While the island of Ihuru made a good base, being small enough to walk around in ten minutes did not make for a lot of interest after a day or two. Also, the management needed to be straightened out about one thing. While the staff ate delicious fish *rotis*, we poor European guests were served Spam as though it were the food of the gods. Apparently the locals envied anything that was imported and came in a tin, seeing it as a luxury. So we were treated to Spam for a day while the staff ate their stewed tuna on a pancake. However ,we soon put them straight and breakfast thereafter was fish *rotis* for all who asked for it.

There are two kinds of tourist island in the Maldives. Those that are in the middle of an atoll are completely sheltered and therefore any diving around the island tends to be tame beginner's territory. If you want serious snorkelling before breakfast each morning, the answer is to pick one of the islands on the edge of an atoll. These will have a jetty and calm water on one side, and reef with a real drop-off and real fish on the other - much more exciting, especially if you are going to be stuck on a postage stamp for a week or more. Frankly, I would advise no more than two or three days on one island, then maybe a boat trip lasting several days, then a few days on another island, if you can still face yet another tropical island paradise.

COCOS KEELING ISLANDS

I was lucky enough to be invited to stay by one of the Australians posted to work on the remote Cocos atoll. Without such an invitation it isn't possible to go there - or at least it wasn't then. Even so, it was a complicated affair involving getting a visa via a personal visit in Perth, then catching the weekly charter flight. It was all worth it, though.

What I saw was a small island in the middle of transition. Clunies-Ross, the man whose family had ruled this island as a personal fiefdom for 150 years, was on the plane out. He had just received several million dollars in compensation from the Australian government for the island, complete with several hundred until recently still-indentured Malay labourers. This workforce had worked the Clunies-Ross plantations in return for housing and subsistence, and latterly for wages issued in Clunies-Ross' own currency and redeemable only in his own store on the island

When I arrived, Clunies-Ross had given up everything except for his large plantation house on Home Island on the other side of the two mile wide lagoon across from West Cocos, where all the Australians lived. The Malay population who still inhabited Home Island were a delightful group to meet, having had almost no contact with the outside world for 150 years. They lived in their simple *kampong* with its rows of neatly kept thatched houses. They welcomed visitors into their homes and with the help of a translator happily answered questions about their lives. If this was the end of feudalism in action, however paternalistic, it must have had a very positive side to it. There was no crime on the island and I saw nothing but smiles when I said hello.

Now that these people have been suborned by the Australian government (cash, free boats, free fuel and free trips to Perth) and have opted for integration with Australia, I doubt whether they are remotely as happy. At the time, the Australians were urgently trying to persuade them to vote in the coming referendum (UN-supervised) to join Australia, as the Russians, after a cooling with the Seychelles, were looking for an Indian Ocean naval base to rival the Americans' on Diego Garcia.

I had plans to visit the island of North Keeling, uninhabited and some 15 miles away, when the Australian governor of Cocos Keeling banned my visit. He would give me no reason, but I soon learnt that a Russian warship was in the vicinity. You only had to look at the Cocos lagoon to realise that with a bit of dredging it would make the best harbour in the Indian Ocean, and with the referendum vote looming, the Australians (and presumably the Americans) didn't want to give the unworldly Malay people of Cocos the chance to vote for independence - in case later, in their innocence, they were bought by the Russians with more boats and free trips than the Australians could afford to give them.

So much for *realpolitik* in the Indian Ocean. I loved the snorkelling on Cocos but regretted never getting to North Keeling Island.

Possibly the best day I spent in this strange group of islands was on Direction Island. It has a beautiful sandy beach on the leeward side that is almost always empty, though it's here that you'll find any passing yachts going round the world. Here during the Second World War an acquaintance of mine helped to bury two British servicemen who had been killed in a shark (probably a tiger shark) attack. (It's extremely unusual for more than one person to be killed at a time.)

With Mark, my seven-year-old son, I went snorkelling in the hope of seeing serious sharks, but we only managed to find numerous black tip reef sharks and one solitary white tip shark.

CHRISTMAS ISLAND

A strange island between Cocos Keeling and Perth, Christmas Island has few if any redeeming features. For a start, there are no beaches, since the island is all cliffs round the outside. And the locals are all seemingly unemployed and supported by the Australian state. What I saw of them augured badly for the delightful people of Cocos Keeling, if this is what full integration had in store for them.

CHAPTER NINE
MIDDLE EAST

ISRAEL

Israel was one of my biggest disappointments. I should have been moved by the fact that it was Holocaust Remembrance Day when I arrived in Tel Aviv. The place was full of survivors and their families, over from New York on a charter flight for the occasion, and the whole thing of being there at that time, and reading the sad notices on the boards, put a bit of a damper on my visit and left me feeling collectively guilty for being alive.

Tel Aviv

Tel Aviv has a scrappy seafront a bit like Durban in South Africa. There are tawdry high rises, hotels and apartments everywhere, and while the sea is warm much of the year, and I was even able to surf there, it isn't really my kind of sea - the water isn't clear and the waves have no force.

The whole town has a somewhat jerry-built feel to it - it looks as though it has been built to look a bit dilapidated from day one. You don't get many smiles in the shops - in fact none so far as I could tell - but maybe you have to speak Hebrew to get treated well.

Jerusalem

Jerusalem was another disappointment. The sheer confusion of the place is bewildering, with Arabs thrusting souvenirs of the Crucifixion at you as you make your way up the alley with the stations of the cross. When you get to the top and enter the church that stands on Calvary Hill, there is money to be handed out - I can't remember if it's for a compulsory cloth to wrap around you or someone to guard your shoes. Once inside, control seems to be in the hands of Coptic Christians from Ethiopia, who will not let you through until you have made a donation. Then there's payment for something else - I think it's to walk around the spot where the one true cross is deemed to have stood.

The best thing in Jerusalem is the Mount of Olives, if only because it's a peaceful spot from which to view this confusing town without actually having to be in it.

Bethlehem

Bethlehem was no better. There was more religious confusion that could damage your faith. Here you were required to wear a skull cap to enter the holy of holies. However the skull cap rental business seemed to be an entirely Muslim monopoly at the entrance, and quite a competitive one at that.

The hinterland

I haven't seen the rest of Israel and perhaps if I had been to other places I would have come away with a more favourable view. Certainly the departure from Tel Aviv Airport left a lasting impression, as I was in a group of about eight and we were all interrogated separately by the security police to ensure that our stories tallied and we were not part of a hijacking team. Better safe than sorry.

CHAPTER TEN
PACIFIC

New Zealand

New Zealand cities, on the whole, are best avoided, including Wellington, though the capital has come up recently, just as Auckland has sunk lower. Forget about Christchurch, the England of the south. The park in the middle is pretty and that's about it. However, the best drive in New Zealand is from Christchurch across the southern plains and hills through Punaki to Queenstown. Go late in the afternoon when the weather is clear, preferably in spring or autumn. You won't regret it. The view is breathtaking.

I remember Rotorua years ago when New Zealanders actually still went there for their Easter holidays. Now it's a tourist trap a couple of miles long, where the Maori culture is the pastiche variety that survives in hotel dance troupes, and tattoos are painted on and washed off each day. You'll probably see ten tourists for every New Zealander, white or brown, that you'll see in Rotorua. If you want to see real Maoris, go to East Cape, where they're genuinely friendly if you stop for a chat. There is a big difference these days between urban and rural Maori. The latter are approachable and friendly. The former are definitely not.

Auckland

Once a fine colonial city built around a beautiful harbour, Auckland has gone downhill in recent years. The downtown area in particular is a mess, with trashy souvenir and fast-food shops and indiscriminate junk architecture and motorways ruining what was once a pleasant city centre. The general impression is one of failed urban planning. Even the sprawling university has little in its appearance to redeem it except nearby Albert Park.

Auckland, once a white bastion, is now heavily populated with Asians and Polynesians. The former are a boon to the community, while the latter, particularly the indigenous Maori, appear to be central to a growing crime problem. The suburbs, on the other hand, are bland and best left to the cars that are an ever-present nuisance and source of pollution. I spend quite a lot of time in New Zealand and try to follow my own advice when in Auckland - get out of town as fast as possible.

Northland

This is by far the prettiest part of the North Island's mainland, and the Bay of Islands rightly figures on most tourist itineraries. Fortunately, it is still relatively unspoilt, though you're best to visit outside the peak local holiday period from Christmas to the end of January. For my money, the best places are even further north. Places such as Taupo Bay on the east coast. You'll still find the feel of the old New Zealand around spots like Runganunu and right up around North Cape. The only other part of the North Island that still has that feel is the small towns round the end of East Cape, on the east side of the North Island.

Great Barrier Island

This is the real gem for North Island visitors. Only two hours from Auckland by fast ferry (or 30 minutes in a plane), Great Barrier has not been visited by most locals or tourists. It has one of the world's finest small boat harbours (Port Fitzroy) and possibly New Zealand's best white-sand ocean beach (Medlands). There are bush walks in the mountainous north, places to eat or stay (try friendly self-catering Mount Saint Paul Estate - tel (09) 4290 994, fax (09) 4290 094). The whole feeling is New Zealand pre-World War Two, and that can only be a good thing in this day and age.

PACIFIC

Queenstown

As a tourist attraction, Queenstown is to the South Island what the Bay of Islands is to the north. It's a pretty lakeside town that's grown a bit too big. If you've visited the Rockies, it will remind you of places like Jasper or Banff. The whole town is built around tourism and personally I prefer nearby Wanaka and Te Anau, both jumping-off points for the many action activities in this region. The Milford Track, the Routeburn Track and Milford Sound feature heavily on the South Island tourist trail, but if you've got the time and money, boating in some of the further afield fjords is well worth it, and there are plenty of trails to walk that won't cost as much or be as booked as the Milford and the Routeburn - the Greenstone and Keppler Tracks, for example.

AUSTRALIA

Perth

The desert around Perth is a lot more interesting than the city of Perth itself. Perth is clean and even pretty in places, especially the river, but in the end there is only one word for it - boring. The wine-growing area to the south, round Margaret River and further south towards Cape Lewin, however, is both beautiful and interesting.

Sydney

Sydney is somewhere I've passed through on and off over the years. It got a lot of publicity in recent years, with the build-up to the Olympics and the Millennium. Some may be hype, but a lot of it is justified. Of course, most of Sydney stretches for what seems like hundreds of miles north, south and west, and is never seen by visitors. But if we're talking about the Sydney that visitors see, there's much that's worth a few days' stay. Some of the beaches to the north are pretty, especially Manly. The harbour itself and its headlands are spectacular. Bondi has been downmarket for many years and is getting worse. I wouldn't go to Sydney to go shopping, though it's along Oxford Street, especially on Saturday when the market is open, that you'll find the most interesting things to buy. Most of Sydney's many galleries are in this area or fairly close. I've actually been to an opera in the Opera House and the standard was high. However, you can join a tour and see inside anyway without having to pay for a performance.

Sydney is the undisputed capital of what has become known as 'Pacific Rim cuisine' - largely the result of mixing seafood and the Oriental immigration wave with a bit of marketing, a dash of flair and some experimentation with food combos that would make a French chef's hair stand on end. Some of the best new restaurants are to be found around the Rocks, many of them in the open air along the quay. Prices, though, are high, even by Sydney standards.

Nowadays Sydney challenges San Francisco as the gay capital of the world. If you're into that sort of thing, the end of February is the time to be there for the gay and lesbian Mardi Gras, especially the annual parade along Oxford Street.

There are plenty of hotels to choose from in Sydney and enough healthy competition to ensure that prices are reasonable. Currently the Rocks, between the Harbour Bridge and the Opera House, is the pleasantest area to stay in and eat out. One outstanding hotel in this area is the Harbour Rocks Hotel, where the manageress is English and really knows a thing or two about service.

North from Sydney

There are many small townships up the coast as you head north towards Queensland. (You could visit the pleasant wine-growing region of the Hunter Valley on the way. It's about 50 miles north of Sydney.) The one that has become best known in the last 30 years is Byron Bay. Once the haunt of hippies and surfers, this beautiful coastal area now attracts visitors of all types. Further north I would suggest you avoid the Gold Coast area (just north of the border with Queensland) and likewise the dreadful Surfer's Paradise, Australia's answer to the Costa del Sol.

After that comes Brisbane, a large humid city built over a humid river that makes the climate unbearable in the summer months. Many visitors head for the coast 50 miles further north at Noosa, a series of pretty bays much loved by surfers and now a haven for retirees with a taste for condominium living. Go to Noosa in March when the crowds have gone but it's still warm, and you'll find the closest Australia has yet come to European sophistication. The shops, the cafes and the boardwalk are all a pleasant change from the rest of Australia, with the possible exception of the cosmopolitan Rocks area in Sydney.

NEW CALEDONIA

A big island (some 100 miles in length), New Caledonia has considerable mineral resources that have made the French reluctant to grant independence despite native uprisings over the years. The island has limited facilities for tourists around Noumea, the capital, and there is the nearby Ile des Pins that has been a luxury resort for 40 years.

I first visited New Caledonia as a student studying French in 1962. The place was a paradise to a 19-year-old unused to tropical islands, Cambodian food (there were several Cambodian families with small restaurants on the island) and sexy French girls. When I returned years later, my perspective had changed and I had been all over the world. The charms of New Caledonia, as a result, looked far more parochial. In the meantime the local Melanesian population, once so friendly despite a century or more of exploitation, had finally had a sense of humour crisis and it was wise to stay out of their way in case they mistook you for an off-duty gendarme and bashed your head in - something that they were fond of doing to the occasional early explorer if local taboos were violated.

The main beach at Anse Vata that was once so appealing had lost its charm by my second visit, and despite all those happy memories from my first five-week stay, I would not put New Caledonia on my revisiting list.

FIJI

Fiji is somewhere I like, without being fanatical about it. I've been there four times and got to know the Yasawa Islands and the offshore island of Tavarua, as well as the main island of Viti Levu. The nice thing about Fiji is that tourism has not gone to its head. It's undoubtedly the most successful tourist group of islands in the Pacific, after Hawaii. Yet for all that, the Melanesian people seem to have hung on to their smiles. They love to dance and sing and, even when putting it on for the tourists, they seem to put their heart into it - especially in the Yasawas, a group of islands to the north where the people were cannibals right into this century. They are still relatively unspoilt by Western development there, and when I went to stay at the Yasawa Island Lodge on Nacula Island, it was interesting to learn that a percentage of the hotel's income goes compulsorily to a fund in mainland Fiji to be redistributed through tribal elders back in the villages neighbouring the hotel. In other words, this money is ring-fenced in the strictest possible way, and this process is going on all over Fiji wherever there is tourist development.

Tavarua is a tiny island that you can walk round in 15 minutes. It is famous among surfers for a spot called Cloudbreak on its fringing reef, half a mile from shore. Everyone going there tends to be a surfer willing to pay a hefty premium for the privilege of surfing uncrowded waves off a private island. If you surf - fine. If you don't, this island definitely isn't worth the high price.

The main island of Viti Levu is not much to look at, which is why all recent development has been on off-shore islands. Once there was only one tourist hotel on Viti Levu - the Korolevu Beach Hotel. Today there are many, despite the poor general quality of the beaches on the mainland. The most developed islands, and some of them are tiny and overdeveloped, are just offshore from Nadi Airport on the west coast. The Yasawa Islands, in contrast, are a half-hour flight to the north and their two hotels tend to be expensive. Other islands further north are being developed and some of these too are in the luxury category. The Yasawa Island Lodge has the biggest bungalows I have seen anywhere and some of the best food you are likely to encounter on a tropical island anywhere, thanks to its top Swiss chef. The snorkelling on the huge coral heads about 200 metres directly out from the Lodge is world class, which is not true of the scuba diving in these islands, at least to judge from the dive I did with the local divemaster.

Fiji rates as possibly the friendliest touristically developed tropical island group in the world. That's really saying something, considering that tourist development is usually synonymous with disaffected locals.

SOCIETY ISLANDS

Tahiti

Tahiti gets the biggest thumbs-down of any island I know. The locals are mostly unhelpful to the point of rudeness, especially the taxi drivers. There are almost no beaches and those that there are consist of black sand. The fringing reef is so far offshore that you basically need a boat to get to it. The hotels are overpriced and so short of sand that generally it is imported to create artificial beaches. The only place apart from China where I have ever had my luggage broken into is the most expensive hotel in Tahiti. There are traffic jams in town in the rush hour. All in all, Tahiti, which I have visited three times over the years, has each time failed to stir any feelings of enjoyment and gone from bad to worse with each successive visit. Even the Gauguin Museum, otherwise interesting, doesn't contain a single original painting by Gauguin. He got out of Tahiti too, in the end, and moved to the Marquesas.

Moorea

Moorea is only a few miles away from Tahiti, but is otherwise completely different. While not all smiles, there is less open antipathy towards Europeans. The island is fairly small and spectacularly mountainous. It was here (and also in Malaysia) that the Fifties film *South Pacific* was shot. The diving is not only good but close inshore. There are plenty of hotels and good beaches, some on islets not far offshore. While I'd get bored spending more than a few days in a place like this, it should be an essential part of a trip round the islands of the Society group.

Raiatea

This island seemed to me a bit boring. There isn't much in the way of nice beaches, though the diving off the reef, a few hundred yards offshore, is good. However, I cannot speak badly of the locals here, as it was on Raiatea that I made friends with an elderly local

man and he lent me his outrigger canoe to paddle the
half mile to the reef with my surfboard. On my return he
made us both lunch in his hut. He opened a tin of sar-
dines, which seemed to be all the food he had, and I felt
I should take back all the things I had ever said about
the people of these islands being so unfriendly. After all,
locals are only unfriendly for a reason, and usually it's
because of some history of exploitation, generally of the
colonial variety. Certainly that tends to be the case in the
Society Islands, where there is the additional factor of
the French military presence over many years and a history of hostility, sometimes violent, between military
and local people. French Polynesia has, after all, been
subjected to dozens of French nuclear tests in the
Tuamotus, that have driven locals from their homes and
threatened parts of the South Pacific with contamination
for centuries to come.

Huahine

This is my personal favourite among the Society
Islands. When I was there, it had only one hotel and
we made a point of not staying in it. Instead we hired a
thatched bungalow by the beach and - if you didn't
mind the rats at night - it was perfectly adequate. But
best of all, it had amazing snorkelling on the drop-off a
mere 100 yards out in front - schools of big fish in close.

Huahine had no tourism to speak of and probably has
little now. But it had more archaeology to offer than the
other islands put together, even the remains of the stone
platforms where the Polynesian kings once held court.
There's a Chinese store down by the dock that sells
everything, and nearby the biggest mango tree you are
likely to see anywhere. On the other side of the island is
a small convent run by French and Tahitian nuns, who
occasionally take in visitors and are very friendly. It's
quite a big island so a rental car is a definite advantage.

Bora Bora

I can only describe Bora Bora as overrated, thanks partly to all the hype surrounding the equally overrated Hotel Bora Bora, which costs a king's ransom to stay at and caters mainly for the Japanese. The food is nondescript considering what you are charged for it. The bicycles they rent out to guests, on the other hand, are kept in good condition and with one you can cycle round the island in about three hours. On the windward side you won't meet a soul, though there isn't an awful lot to see.

To be fair to the hotel, the bungalows are reasonably comfortable, and the staff do make an effort to be polite, though their helpfulness doesn't come from the heart, and it shows. Obviously you can only take staff training so far in the Society Islands.

As usual in these islands, the locals are not a bundle of laughs, and are unlikely even to return a smile. Prices are high and there are virtually no beaches. The beach in front of the Hotel Bora Bora is of the reconstructed variety and to reach the reef you have to swim in water two feet deep for more than half a mile. The drop-off on the far side, however, is good, as it tends to be all over the Society Islands if you are bold enough to swim that far and then go out through a pass in the reef to the deeper water, where it starts to get interesting.

The main lagoon is best viewed from a boat from out to sea and the best way to do this is by taking the ferry from Bora Bora to one of the other islands. To while away the time on these trips, the locals tend to sit around on the deck eating, drinking and singing. There is usually someone with a good voice and a guitar among them.

In fact, take one of the inter-island ferries, as I have done occasionally, and you will get your best chance to break the ice with the otherwise taciturn Polynesians. Believe me, the ice can be broken but you have to work at it. Share some food and join in the singing, sitting cross-legged on a ferry deck, and you stand your best chance.

TUAMOTU ISLANDS

This cluster of coral atolls is an astonishing sight from the air, every one of hundreds of coral heads inside the inner lagoons being clearly defined as if there were no water below at all, merely a light blue canvas. Yet this water is likely to be 20 or more feet deep. It travels through wide passes in the reef with the rising and falling tide and it is here that fish of all types and particularly grey sharks congregate to feed. I visited Rangiroa, the best known of the Tuamotus, and made sure I dived in a couple of these passes. In the first pass (Avatoru Pass) I free-dived in about 50 feet of water and realised that I would see a lot more with scuba.

So the same afternoon I joined a scuba group and dived on the rising tide in the best known pass (Tiputa Pass), in about 80 feet of water. The sight of a wall of several hundred dogfish and behind them a dozen or so larger sharks (grey sharks up to two metres) is impressive from a distance of about 20 yards, particularly as there was a large school of barracuda directly above us and several leopard rays gliding around nearby. However, the culmination of the dive was the sight of a pod of some half dozen wild dolphin, from mature males about four metres long to a baby about one metre in length, idling past us almost within touching distance before swimming off straight over the top of the nearby sharks.

There isn't much else to do on Rangiroa. Bicycle is the way to get around and it's all pretty hot work. There are a few small beach hotels to stay at, but I would spend only a couple of days here before moving on, as we did, to the Marquesas.

MARQUESAS ISLANDS

The Marquesas group is nothing like the Society Islands or the Tuamotus. Although they all form part of French Polynesia, the distances are large. For example the Tuamotus are about 500 miles from Tahiti and the Marquesas another 500 further still. Gauguin died in the Marquesas, having been kicked out of Tahiti for lewd behaviour, and the French poet and song writer Jacques Brel is buried here. Thor Heyerdahl spent his honeymoon year with his first wife on Fatu Hiva in 1947 and found the inspiration here for his Kon Tiki expedition.

We spent several days on Nuku Hiva, an island which inspired a novel by Herman Melville about the local cannibals, and entranced Robert Louis Stevenson with the beauty of one of its beaches. We didn't have a boat and land travel is difficult and expensive - we're talking up to $100 for a transfer from hotel to airport. The people we encountered were friendly and we were left with the suspicion that their good humour had been bought with lavish handouts from the EU's development funds. While many seemed to be unemployed, there was no shortage of shiny new four-wheel drive cars and every house had a TV set. The main township of Taiohae doesn't have a lot to excite the visitor, apart from a good takeaway food stall on the seafront. You can walk over the hill to a bay and have the stony beach all to yourself for a day's swimming. Or on the headland in front of the town you can dive and find plenty of hammerhead sharks to swim among, if the fancy takes you.

We took a trip with others over to the north side of the island and visited Anaho bay, where Stevenson got so ecstatic. It was pretty and the hills behind made for a spectacular backdrop, but the snorkelling was poor and, all in all, I could have pointed Stevenson in the direction of prettier bays, in Moorea for example.

The views in the Marquesas are spectacular where

they look across the sea to the other islands in the group, with their strangely formed volcanic peaks often piercing the clouds. Ua Pou, in particular, makes a spectacular focal point when you look straight out to sea from Taiohae. There are a few places to stay that are little more than home-stays, though at the Keikahanui Inn, where we were, the food was excellent, cooked by a Frenchman. The owner, Rose Corser, was an American widow who had sailed in with her yachtsman husband years before and decided to stay. The truth is, I was getting bored after a couple of days, despite the tales of cannibals and their ceremonial sites which still survive.

COOK ISLANDS

Rarotonga is the principal island in this group, which is spread over a large expanse of the Pacific. You can go round Rarotonga in a couple of hours on a bike. The island is one of those volcanic ones where the road goes round the edge and the interior is all mountainous slopes and largely unreachable without heroic effort in the heat. We opted for the cowardly route and stuck to the coast. There is a strong evangelical streak among the local Polynesians here, as on many Pacific islands, with the result that doing anything very vigorous on a Sunday is frowned on. I was keen to surf one Sunday and had to be pretty discreet about it. The Royal Rarotongan remains the best hotel, though there is a spot further round called Muri Lagoon that is much prettier. It has some inshore islands and the snorkelling conditions are better there. When all's said and done, though, Rarotonga is just plain boring.

WESTERN SAMOA

Not to be confused with American Samoa, Western Samoa is really two islands, Upolu and Savai'i, linked by a ferry service. The more developed and less interesting of the islands is Upolu. Its landmarks include Vailima, the final home of Robert Louis Stevenson, and Aggie Grey's, once a notorious watering hole for the wilder element among South Seas travellers - the sort of place that only had Quinn's in Papeete to rival it for notoriety. Today it is a sedate hotel on the outskirts of Apia, the capital. You can have a drink and nibble sandwiches by the pool and wonder how it must have been in the good old, bad old days.

The north side of Upolu has the odd hotel and some very dangerous lagoon snorkelling that is not for the inexperienced. Two US servicemen had gone out there in a pedalo a week before we arrived and were never seen again. I went in to see what the risks were and found that when the tide went out, the current sweeping through the lagoon towards the pass where water exits to the sea was the strongest I had encountered anywhere, in years of snorkelling around passes in coral lagoons.

More interesting is Savai'i. Here we stayed in the local visitors' house in a village ruled by a headman. We attended a local church service. The Polynesians love to sing and they do it well. The singing was memorable, though the people seemed more interested in our presence than in the gospel that Sunday, as visitors to the island were few and far between. We went fishing with the locals and managed to catch a lot of skipjack tuna, so we had *sashimi* for dinner that night and the locals received a large pile of fish for all the village. After that we got smiles everywhere we went, until one of the women in our group dared to walk through the village street in shorts on a Sunday. Not a good move. The anger of some of the elders was quickly communicated and the same mistake was not made again. Apparently shorts were not a problem on the other days of the week.

Savai'i has underground caves to explore, dangerous when your only torch is a lighted paper wick stuffed into the end of a bottle filled with paraffin. There are mountain pools and a waterfall where you can swim. Also some of the most dangerous body-surfing territory I have ventured into, and some of the heaviest reef surf. I still have an injured shoulder muscle seven years later.

As South Pacific trips go, this was one of the best.

TONGA

I had expected more of Nuku Alofa, the capital. It is a desultory place with no endearing features, not even the natives. There are no interesting beaches that I saw. We flew from here to Vava'u in the north, to pick up a charter yacht. On the way, we stopped briefly in the Ha'apai atoll where there are dozens of small islands, and with hindsight I think this would have been more interesting sailing territory. There are now quite a lot of boats around the Vava'u group, though many of them belong to people, mainly Americans, sailing across the Pacific.

The best thing about being on a boat in the Pacific is rowing over and talking to other sailors, though I always feel a bit of a cheat as I've inevitably flown in and chartered a boat, instead of spending months and years doing things the hard way. Off one small island in the Vava'u group there are usually a number of boats heading down the milk run from California and Hawaii through Tahiti and Tonga to New Zealand before the start of the hurricane season. As in the Atlantic, the places that the yachtsmen head for are not the same places that tourists visit. From what I have seen, some of the more interesting Pacific sailors seem to end up in Nuku Hiva in the Marquesas, Huahine in the Society Islands, and Vava'u in Tonga.

One American who invited us over to his boat for a drink on Vava'u had been at it for so many years that he had swapped wives with another sailor along the way and was now completing the voyage with wife number two. However, the prize goes to a German couple we had a drink with in the Marquesas. They had been sailing the world together for 20 years and had still not completed their first circumnavigation.

Even with a boat, the diving was not that impressive around Vava'u. We forgave the locals their seeming coldness, though, at the airport, when my 14-year-old daughter had a small Polynesian baby thrust into her arms by its mother and was asked to take it to her sister in the capital 100 miles away. Fortunately, the sister was waiting to take the uncomplaining baby off us when we arrived.

HAWAII

I have only been to Oahu, the main island in the Hawaiian group. In fact I have been to the airport so many times in the middle of the night on transit stops that I have long ago lost count. However, I have only bothered to really check out the island once, and was so disillusioned that I have not been back since to really visit. Maybe it was the fact that my towel was stolen while I was surfing from the beach at Makaha on the south-west side of Oahu (a spot where *haoles* are few and far between) - but aren't Hawaiians meant to believe that everything belongs to everyone? - so maybe it was only borrowed.

No, the Hawaiians definitely are not fond of *haoles*, the Western invaders who have taken over their islands, though nowadays there are no pure Hawaiians left and most visitors seem to be Japanese.

I cannot like a city like Honolulu, with its traffic and its pollution and its noise. If there is any part of Oahu that is tolerable, it is the more laid-back North Shore between Kahuku Point to the east and Kaena Point to the west. Apart from the attraction of the surf, though, there isn't a lot to do, and from what I hear, the traffic along Kam Highway on the North Shore can be bumper-to-bumper these days.

EASTER ISLAND

It's a long way to go to see a few statues sticking out of the ground. You won't find lots of beaches on Easter Island, either - there's one at Anakena where the main row of statues is, and that's about it. Fortunately, though, the water is warm. The landscape is fairly bleak generally, with just one patch of real trees somewhere in the middle. You can walk down into the volcanic crater on one side of Easter Island, if you fancy the idea of a day's climb up and down slopes to reach a swamp at the bottom. Then there is the township of Hanga Roa itself - more a straggle of houses really, with the odd bar aimed at the football-loving locals. Don't expect good food on Easter Island, especially if you stay in home-stay accommodation as I did. In fact, only Fernando de Noronha off Brazil rates worse in my food and drink league table.

There was surfing to be had, of a kind, on Easter Island. There was transport to get around, in the shape of horses (old nags) for hire, or four-wheelers if you were in a bit of a hurry. How long you stay on Easter Island depends somewhat on the flights between Tahiti and Santiago on LAN Chile Airlines - as far as I know there are still only two or three flights a week. There is supposed to be one comfortable but expensive place to stay but I didn't see it. My advice if you go there is to stay two or three days at the most.

PAPUA NEW GUINEA

PNG doesn't rate highly on most travellers' visiting lists unless they happen to be anthropologists. The capital, Port Moresby, is reckoned to be one of the most dangerous places this side of Chechnya. They say that Fridays are worst as this is pay-day, when everyone gets drunk and goes berserk. My son and I stayed one night in Port Moresby and got out after a quick look around in a taxi, having been warned that it wasn't advisable to go about on foot. From what I saw, we didn't miss much.

We flew to Mount Hagen in the middle of the island, by now reeling from the cost of everything. I have only had that feeling twice before, that this was bankruptcy country if you stayed too long - in Sweden and in Japan. The price of a motel room in Mount Hagen seemed to run into thousands of dollars, but it probably wasn't quite that bad. However, there was nothing much to see except a lot of locals with teeth and gums bright red from chewing betel nut.

So from there we flew in a de Havilland Twin Otter to Madang. We were lucky to arrive at all: when our bush pilot flew us out of a cloud, we looked out to see the top of a mountain about 30 feet below us. Even the pigs at the back of the plane squealed at that point.

Madang was as boring as the rest, apart from the sight of thousands of fruit bats hanging from a tree.

On to the Admiralty Islands, a couple of hundred miles offshore in Micronesia, and at last things started to look up. We stayed with an old Australian who had fall- en off a ship nearby in the dim and distant past and been there ever since. Now he had a thriving local business and collected seashells. He proudly showed us his three rare golden cowries. Apparently they are worth thou- sands. To me they just looked like pretty shells. His son took us scuba diving and we got to encounter some large black tip reef sharks close up down at about 100 feet - maybe 20 of them within touching distance, and some a couple of metres in length. That alone made our short stay on the Admiralty Islands worthwhile. What we didn't see, and it was probably just as well, was a 20- foot sea-going crocodile that was said to swim along the coast now and again.

POSTSCRIPT

Traveller's Rest

Can you ever get tired of travelling? In fact the answer is 'yes'. I've been hard at it, travelling, for over 30 years - long enough to see changes, and virtually all of them for the worse.

The big one is traffic. There are still places where there are good roads and no cars to speak of (the country roads in New Zealand's South Island are probably one of the best examples). In the UK, traffic congestion is rapidly heading for the top of the political agenda. In London, the number of children suffering from asthma as a result of pollution goes on rising. What is happening now in the so-called developed world is what will be happening 20 years later in the developing world, or in some cases has already happened.

Take Bangkok as possibly the worst example, though I've heard that Lagos is at crisis point. I was in Bangkok recently and I spent more time watching TV in my hotel room than I did out and about on the streets. That would normally have been unthinkable, but now I suffer from upper bronchial congestion induced by long stays in London, and Bangkok was only making it worse. The culprit in both cases is PM10 and the even more noxious PM2.5, diesel pollutants spewed daily into the atmosphere by the ton in all crowded cities, quite apart from all that carbon monoxide.

Global warming looks as though it is here to stay, and while some may welcome a Mediterranean climate on British shores, the fact is that traffic pollution makes it worse, even if the root cause turns out to be sunspots or whatever natural theory you adhere to.

So where are the places to go that have the cleanest air and are least likely to send you spluttering to your air-conditioned hotel room?

I've mentioned one already and that is New Zealand, but I have a soft spot for New Zealand generally, since its old-fashioned ways are a big plus point. Equally interesting is the north-west of Scotland. The roads may be narrow, but at least they aren't sunken the way they are in Cornwall - so you always get a view.

Try the road to the Isles out of Oban and up via Ullapool, round the tip of Scotland and along the north coast of Sutherland to John O'Groats in Caithness, and on down the coast to Thurso. Do it in mid-September in Indian summer weather. The effect is breath-taking as you pass some of the most beautiful coastal scenery in the world - clear blue (but cold) water and white sandy beaches in the north-west, interlinked with ancient lochs and ruins.

I don't like tropical countries a lot. I don't like the temperature much over 70 degrees and I don't like high humidity. So why do I go to tropical islands more than anywhere else? The answer has to lie somewhere in my primordial past when all our ancestors lived in the sea. I just can't get enough of the stuff. I dive, I sail, I surf, I windsurf, I swim. So when I get the urge still to travel - and I do still get it - it's really the urge to get into the sea. But I hate cold water, so I end up going to hot tropical places just for the pleasure of spending hours at a time in the oh-so-pleasant sea.

You won't catch me roasting on the beach, though. For me, it's out of the water and into the shade as fast as possible.

I don't like crowds - they make me feel claustrophobic. I once went to the Notting Hill Carnival and I got the feeling so strongly that I've avoided crowds ever since. But most of the time, a crowd for me is anything over about two people, and even then I've got to know the other person.

Well maybe I'm exaggerating a bit, but my idea of a day spoilt is finding a lonely white sand beach on a coral island (see San Salvador above) and looking up to see another traveller coming along the beach. Locals are fine

197

- I like locals and it's their place after all. But show me another visitor on my beach and I'm off in search of somewhere else to call my own.

That may sound greedy but it's a fact that people follow each other lemming-like to the same spots, leaving most of the world's attractive shorelines empty, even in this overcrowded day and age. We're not just talking about far-flung islands. Right here in the United Kingdom there are miles of empty coastline at the height of summer, if only you'll look for it. A spot right in the middle of the Dorset coast comes to mind, and a memory of swimming there naked on the hottest day of the summer in 1994.

The reason for all these empty beauty spots is that not only do people follow each other - they also don't like walking to get to a place they can call their own for a day. If they can't get to it within 100 yards of the car park, they ain't going. Well that's fine by me, as I like to walk, and walking a mile or three to find a beach to myself is all part of the fun.

There's no denying that a lot of countries would rather not have any foreign tourists at all, if it weren't for the hard currency they bring in. Sometimes they discover that tourism is such a jackpot that they get greedy and dive in headlong. There are places where tourism is the number one earner of foreign exchange: Mallorca, Venice, Bermuda, Hawaii, Nassau, Kenya, Tunisia - to name a few.

As far back as the Sixties, some countries were waking up to the fact that if you want the revenues but not the people, one solution is to try and get a few high-spending individuals rather than a horde of penniless yahoos. This approach was practised rigorously by Bhutan from the Seventies onwards, with a requirement that all visitors spend a (high) minimum amount per day in hard currency. Twenty years ago in Bhutan, it was $250 per day, which was quite a lot at the time.

More recently, Mallorca has tried to turn its back on the mass market in a belated and seemingly half-hearted attempt to stop the rot. However, the horse in this particular case seems to have already bolted, and for all their effort to cut down traffic congestion and clean the roadsides and the sea, it just isn't enough. Mallorca gets English package holiday visitors, but the real money comes from the Germans buying property there and keeping their gin palace boats in Palma's marinas.

This brings me to another phenomenon. When enough tourists come to a place, especially if they buy land or retire there, you get a new kind of colonisation. It doesn't usually cover whole countries. In the case of Spain, it's the Germans in Mallorca. But the British are doing the same around Marbella, the Dordogne, Provence and Tuscany. The Swedes long ago took over the Gambia, and everybody and his cat has taken over the Canary Islands (though the battle between the Germans and the Brits goes one way or the other depending on which island you're talking about). Then there are British enclaves in Florida and Cape Town, and the numbers of Brits in Barbados seemed to threaten for a while to relieve the place of its independence from the old mother country.

What we are witnessing is the beginning of a trend that will expand as the new century advances. Large numbers of the more affluent will migrate towards the sun, either to retire or to work on a full-time basis. If working from home in the cyberworld of the internet really does happen, and international communication costs get even lower, I would say that there is going to be considerably more of this neo-colonisation, and to destinations further flung than just Europe, Florida and the Caribbean.

This is all good news for the welcoming destination, until development reaches the level it has in Florida and Mallorca and people start to complain. Meanwhile the first colonists have already moved on somewhere else and are pioneering a new place to get away from it all in the sun.

Let's speculate on where these new destinations might be, once the locals have started burning down British properties in Tuscany and Provence. In general it seems to be the places that are most popular as a holiday destination that become the target for the timeshare set and maybe even the buyers and builders of serious villas. On that basis, you would expect there to be a rush for, say, Mauritius or St Lucia or even Queensland.

Well, I haven't been to St Lucia or Mauritius for over ten years, and in those days it was all a matter of holidays only - not living there. But I have been to Queensland recently, and if a place on the coast like Noosa is typical, the phenomenon is indeed showing signs of happening down under. Friends of mine have just bought an apartment there, but are actually spending most of their year in that other new colony - Costa Rica - discovered by Americans and Canadians and most of Europe except, strangely enough, the British.

For my money, though, I think it won't take the British long to discover Costa Rica, as the Swiss in particular have already done - perhaps because Costa Rica has always been known as the Switzerland of Central America.

So there you have the four biggies as far as predictions go. My money is on Costa Rica, St Lucia, Mauritius and Queensland. Mind you, I wouldn't live in any of them. They're better than old colonies like Florida, Marbella and Mallorca, but they don't have the charm of Tuscany or Provence. I almost forgot - there's the island of Provo in the Turks and Caicos islands, another place destined for stardom, though starting with the American market. Great diving, but would you seriously want to live there?

There isn't much point in asking me where I would go and build my hideaway, because I don't like civilisation all that much, and most neo-colonisers do. If I had to live all year on one Caribbean island, I'd probably go for Dominica, provided I had a boat to travel around with, since the roads are so bad. But Dominica wouldn't be most people's cup of tea, as the beaches are all black sand. What appeals to me is the wildness of the place, the absence of visitors and the seriously unspoilt snorkelling off the windward coast.

But if I had to choose a luxurious developed Caribbean island and I had infinite money, I would probably go for St Barths. If I wanted good beaches and a civilised but unspoilt island, I'd choose Anguilla, while I'd opt for Anegada in the BVI if I were looking for endless days of lotus-eating on a flat and dry coralline island with outstanding snorkelling.

In the Indian Ocean I'd opt for Rodrigues, and in the Pacific it would have to be the Yasawa Islands north of Fiji, not least because the Melanesian peoples of the Pacific are without doubt a good deal more friendly than the Polynesians on the islands further east.

The whole world is going to be shaken up in the next hundred years as the distinction blurs between visiting a place on holiday and actually living there. More and more of the affluent in northern Europe and North America will end up following the sun and migrating between homes in both hemispheres in order to have an endless summer. In this way, Australia and New Zealand will experience a boom in people who live there half the year.

The greed of the local Mr Big's who control everything, including the goverment and the banks in most developing countries, will ensure that the Mallorca phenomenon has no problem spreading. The chance to make money will oil the wheels of local bureaucracy and leave the fat cats, who own what used to be worthless bits of coastal land, laughing all the way to the bank. There will be token gestures in the direction of planning, pollution control, traffic congestion, but when all's said and done, money in the right pockets will ensure the continued destruction of all that is best about the planet.

Where is this going to happen next, apart from the places I've already mentioned? Well it's been going on for some time in parts of Mexico, but Nicaragua is just beginning to feel the urge. It could happen in Morocco if the new regime turns out to have a stable future. Believe it or not, if the Libya thing with Gadaffi is ever resolved, you could see a lot of development there. If the Roman ruins in Libya are properly organised like Luxor and such places in Egypt, Libya could really take off. Likewise Syria, if the Middle East ever sorts out its problems. Sri Lanka will one day be seen as stable again and, when that happens, watch out for the development of the beautiful east coast, currently totally undeveloped.

In Australia - and this is long term - the thousands of miles of Indian Ocean coastline stretching far to the north of Perth will one day become another Queensland, so if you fancy a real estate investment for your grandchildren, this might be the place to go for it.

In the Pacific, the next Hawaii is undoubtedly Fiji, thanks to the genuine friendliness of the people. Here the many out islands will see major development over the next 50 years.

And in New Zealand, the best place to buy land, if you still can by the time this is published, is Great Barrier, an island the size of the Isle of Wight just 60 miles northeast of Auckland. It has 1,800 inhabitants, three small primary schools, shops, accommodation and restaurants, and it can be reached in 20 minutes by daily scheduled flight or in two hours by fast ferry from Auckland - with the chance to spot whales on the way.

The Barrier, as it's known locally, was named by Captain Cook. The way of life is slow and old-fashioned and that's how the locals want to keep it. You can have a phone and satellite TV there, but you won't find much in the way of culture. However, the charm of the place lies in the friendly locals and their laid-back approach to everything. They even speak English. Great Barrier Island may be about to become the jewel in Auckland's new plan for the islands of the Gulf, and if this happens land will no longer be quite so easy to come by. Be warned though - the New Zealand government doesn't want another Mallorca there, and for that reason they have a law that prevents you from buying more than about one acre on an offshore island unless you're a New Zealand citizen.

I started off by implying that I had lost some of my urge to travel. Maybe I'm jaded just a bit. I've lived through eco-tourism (a bit of an oxymoron if you ask me) and it doesn't seem to have changed anything. I've watched as even Bhutan got more and more coverage on TV and presumably let more people in. Twenty years ago China had just opened up to the West and to go there was still a big deal. Then it was Mustang, the part of Nepal where the people are really Tibetan. Then Tibet itself, or the sanitised ethnically cleansed bits of it that the Peking government would grudgingly let you see for the sake of the dollar income.

Kenya boomed and went, broken by its own corruption and rocketing crime - not a good place to buy a villa after all. South Africa looks like going the same way. The Seychelles took off in the early Seventies, then collapsed and slowly recovered. Sri Lanka simply got dragged down and is only now beginning to get over the Tamil problem. Australia and New Zealand have undoubtedly come of age as tourist destinations, not just as somewhere to go to see the relatives who emigrated in the Fifties. Hawaii became America's Ballearic Islands -

over-exploited. Meanwhile, Europeans discovered the joys of the Canary Islands - even if the sea is a touch frosty in the winter and the wind never stops blowing sand in your face on Fuerteventura.

Turkey became the cheaper (and to my mind better) alternative to Greece for a sun and sea holiday. In the Caribbean, places like Barbados and St Lucia pulled in the British tourist, or, if your budget was more limited, Cuba and the Dominican Republic. If you sailed and were tired of chartering in the Med, suddenly there were boats to be had in the Virgin Islands, the Bahamas, the Seychelles, Tonga, Thailand, the Maldives, and all over Australia and New Zealand. If you skied, there were the Rockies - Canadian or American - and for only about £200 more than going off to the Alps.

All of which suggests that our perception of the world has changed radically in the last 30 years, even though the time is takes to get anywhere is no faster than it was then. In fact, with traffic and airport congestion and the problems of air traffic control, it may even be that it was faster in those days. I have crossed the Pacific many times from Los Angeles to Auckland non-stop and the fastest I ever did it was in 1978 on Pan Am's SP version of the Boeing 747. Yes, the journey was actually faster in those days. Mail between Auckland and London at that time routinely took three days, compared with five days now.

Which only goes to show that the shrinking of the world to a global village isn't all one-way. The final irony may be that all the Concorde aircraft in service today are about to reach the limit of their legal lifespan. When they do and are withdrawn, there will be no more supersonic passenger jets in operation. In other words, flying on some routes at maximum speed will be half as fast as it was 30 years ago.

Wouldn't it be nice if the clock could be turned back in other ways - maybe to the days when everyone travelled by ship? I don't envy those now in their twenties, who never knew the time when the world was a safer and friendlier place to travel in, without traffic congestion or much pollution.

My consolation is that I know I can always find an empty beach somewhere.

Ian Wilson
New Zealand
December 1999